Growing Dahlias

Garden display blooms

The author's garden in autumn

This book is to be returned
the last date stamped be

Growing Dahlias

Gayner W. Parker

Kangaroo Press

Acknowledgements

The author wishes to thank the following:

The Division of Soils, CSIRO for use of the table of plant food deficiency symptoms from their book *Food for Plants*.

The Australian Dahlia Council for use of the information contained in their book *Guide to Dahlias*.

Swami Vinayananda of New Delhi, India for information about latecuttings and flower pot dahlias from his book *Dahlia Growing*.

The America Dahlia Society for the wealth of information on research into various aspects of dahlias provided from time to time by their Bulletins.

Miss Sharon Ruxton for line drawings.

Mr Nev Naumann of Queensland, Mr Jim McLaren of Western Australia, Mr John Menzel and Mr Ray Sellick of South Australia, and Mr George Harding of Tasmania for the loan of colour slides to complement the author's own.

While most of the colour photos in this book were taken by the author, they include not only his own blooms, but many of the better flowers which have been exhibited on show benches and in the gardens of dahlia growers whom he has visited. Many thanks to all concerned.

Cover: 'Gay Sunset' (Medium Semi-cactus type)

Reprinted 1987
First published in 1986 by Kangaroo Press Pty Ltd
3 Whitehall Road (P.O. Box 75) Kenthurst 2156
Typeset by G.T. Setters Pty Ltd
Printed in Hong Kong by Colorcraft Ltd

ISBN 0-86417-077-7

Contents

Introduction

Selection of Cultivars 6

Methods of Propagation 6

History 7

1 Lifting, Dividing and Storing Tubers

Lifting Clumps 8

Dividing Clumps 8

Storing Tubers 9

Building a Glasshouse 9

2 Propagation of Green Plants

Taking Cuttings 10

Planting and Cultivation 10

Potting 11

Latecuttings 11

Labels 14

3 Soil Preparation

Drainage 15

Planting a Green Crop 15

Soil pH Balance 15

Final preparations 16

Colour plates 17

4 Planting

Staking the Bed 33

Planting Tubers 33

Planting Pot Tubers and Green Plants 34

5 Watering

How Plants Use Water 35

Water Needs of Dahlias 35

6 Weed Control 37

7 Feeding the Soil to Supply Plant
Nutrients

The Basic Fertilisers 38

Fertiliser Proportion for Dahlias 38

Application of Fertilisers 38

Plant Food Deficiencies 39

8 Pruning

To Induce New Growth 40

To Shape the Bushes 41

To Increase the Size of Flowers 42

Miniature Flowers 42

Picking Flowers 42

Correcting the Angle of Flowers 43

General Observations 43

9 Tying 45

10 Shading

Making the Shades 46

Positioning the Shades 46

11 Flower Pot Dahlias

Giant and Large Size Cultivars 48

Medium and Small Size Cultivars 48

Miniature and Other Very Small Sizes 49

Cultivation of Flower Pot Dahlias 49

12 Growing Dahlias by the Soilless Method 50

13 Selection of Seed Parents 51

14 Producing and Gathering Seed 52

15 Growing Seedlings 54

16 Pests and Diseases

Pests 55

Diseases 55

17 Exhibiting

Selecting and Cutting Blooms 57

Packing and Transporting Blooms 57

Staging of Blooms 58

Requirements for Flower Pot Dahlias 58

18 Appreciation of Dahlia Blooms 59

Floret Forms as Described by the
Australian Dahlia Council 60

Exhibition Standards for Specimen
Blooms 62

List of Sizes and Types of Dahlias 65

Glossary of Terms 66

Abbreviations 68

Basic Show Schedule 69

Annual Cycle of Dahlia Growing 71

Recommended Cultivars 74

Index 78

Introduction

Dahlias come in a wide variety of sizes and shapes, and these two factors are used to classify them. The size groups cover a range of from under 50 mm to over 260 mm, and are defined by upper and lower limits to diameter. The form groups are based on the shape both of the bloom and of the florets which make up the flowerhead. These are described in the Standard Requirements of Perfection (page 62).

Dahlia flowers also come in an extensive range of colours. Most of the types are available in white, cream, yellow, gold, bronze, pink, lavender, mauve, flame, tangerine, scarlet, red, purple and bi-colours (two distinct colours on each floret with a position on the florets at which the colour changes abruptly), blends (two or more colours which are distinguishable from a distance of two metres and merge into each other) and variegateds (florets have a base colour with a distinctive colour spotted or splashed over it).

Dahlias can be grown for the cut flower trade, garden display or for exhibition purposes. The small flowered cultivars are very prolific and provide a source of flowers throughout their flowering season. They are delightful, delicate and ideal for use on specific occasions as decorations in a hall, church, foyer of an hotel, theatre or similar area. In the garden their range of colours offers an eye-catching display. The dwarf bedding dahlias grown from seed or seedlings such as Cinderella, Hi-Dolly, Unwin's Dwarf Bedding and Collarette mixtures, are very satisfactory for garden borders or beds in public parks. They can be planted close and do not need stakes because they have short stems.

Provided a few basic requirements such as situation, soil preparation, staking, tying and care of the tubers are given due attention, dahlias are very easily grown and the results will be very rewarding.

Selecting Cultivars

When selecting cultivars, it is best to visit growers' and nurserymen's gardens and see the plants in bloom. If your plants are given the same attention, you can expect similar results, provided that your climate is the same. For instance, cultivars do not always flower in exactly the same form in different states or countries. The main thing to be sure of is that the stock is generally healthy and virus-free.

If you are unable to see dahlias growing, visit the autumn flower shows, which are held during March and April, to see them on display; or, if this is not possible, obtain catalogues from nurserymen. These must be studied very carefully when selecting the cultivars you require because the descriptions are usually very brief. Collections are advertised for those who are not so fastidious about quality of bloom but who want a blaze of colour.

There are a number of new cultivars released each year and you can keep adding a few more to your collection to keep it up to date, possibly discarding others to make room for them. In this way your garden continues to provide interest, as you wait for the new cultivars to flower.

Although dahlias are so easy to grow, it is a mistake to be over-enthusiastic and grow too many plants to the detriment of their quality. It is wiser to confine your plantings to the type which appeals to you most, or meets your requirements best.

Methods of Propagation

Seed or seedlings produce a large percentage of plants having blooms which do not conform to the generally accepted standards but which do provide a wealth of colour in the garden. Exceptions to this are the Unwin's Dwarf Bedding, Hi-Dolly, Cinderella and other seeds which produce flowers of a consistent form peculiar to themselves in a wide range of colours. With these latter seedlings, staking is not essential because of their dwarf-growing habit. They are prolific flowerers.

When you purchase dahlias, be they tubers, green plants, or seedlings, provided they are supplied to you in good order and condition, it is your responsibility to care for them adequately and grow them. The multiplication of tubers during the growing season is usually generous, but some cultivars are shy bearers and unless care is taken with these tubers you can easily lose the cultivar.

History

The cultivated dahlia originated from several species native to the higher country of Mexico. These were single, smallish but decorative flowers in red, pink, or white. They were grown by the Aztecs as medicinal plants and possibly flowers of worship, and in the Badianus Manuscript, which was published in 1552, there is an illustration of a dahlia plant which was drawn by an Aztec artist. The dahlia was brought to Europe in 1789 and named after the Swedish botanist, Professor Andreas Dahl.

The first spectacular fully double break occurred in 1814 and many hundreds of cultivars were produced. They were rather stiff, formal, and spherical, generally known as Show dahlias. Bi-coloured cultivars were known as Fancy.

The flat-petalled Decorative dahlias developed later as double forms of *Dahlia rosea* types, and Pompons as small forms of the spherical Show dahlia. The late Mr Norm Williams of New South Wales produced many Pompon dahlias which he named 'Willo', and they have been grown all over the world. In recent years local grower the late Mr H.K. Brand of Croydon introduced many Giant Decoratives to make the name Croydon world renowned. The late Mr R.R. Knight of Mile End, another South Australian veteran, also raised several high-ranking Giant Decoratives including 'The Master'.

Collarette dahlias with their eight flat rounded florets and inner collar of petaloids, originated in the gardens at Lyons, in 1900, under the direction of Professor Gerard. The first Collarette was named 'President Viger'. Some of this type were raised by the late Mr C.B. Weiss of Magill.

The greatest departure of form was with the Cactus dahlia which appeared in 1879. This was named *Dahlia juarezii* after the famous Mexican President Juarez. At first they had weak stems and the flowers hung on the bushes but later stiff-stemmed cultivars were produced. The Large Semi-cactus, half Decorative and half Cactus then emerged, and gradually the Medium Cactus came into being. The late Mr R.E. Ransome of Caul-field, Victoria, and the late Mr Dave Hendry of Kallista, Victoria, raised many Cactus dahlias.

Locally, the late Mr C.B. Weiss, late Mr L.W. Grivell, and the late Mr H. Sudholz raised the well-known 'Koongarra', 'Kensington', and 'Fernie' cultivars respectively.

Then came the Star dahlias, small flowers with florets broad at the base and pointed, arranged in three rows around a clean disc centre. Fully double Stars were introduced in Australia by the late Mr McKenzie of Blackburn, Victoria, and designated Charms in the early 1930s. They are most decorative and free-flowering. I owe my interest in the dahlia to the late Mr W. (Bill) Hughes of Unley who introduced me to these Charms in 1935. Previously I had grown Decorative and Peony types of dahlias.

Naturally, with the growing of Medium and Charm Cactus and Semi-cactus in the same gardens, in the late 1940s the Small Cactus and Semi-cactus followed. As all this was happening to the Cactus dahlias, so the various sizes in the Decorative dahlias were introduced.

The Nymphea type is a more recent introduction.

The raising of seedlings is so fascinating an experience, that most exhibitors of dahlias, as well as nurserymen, have grown them in an attempt to obtain a new cultivar which no other grower has. I have experienced the appearance of Anemone type dahlias in my seedling bed although the seed was taken from Orchid type cultivars. There were no Anemone type dahlias growing in my garden or the gardens of my neighbours. Possibly these seedlings were a throw-back to an earlier parentage in the cultivars producing the seed. As dahlias are hybrids, crossed species of dahlias, they may produce varying types of flowers. Currently, a new type of dahlia which has eight florets like those of the Orchid type and a contrasting coloured collar of florets like the Collarette type has been established in the U.S.A.

When a new type like this one appears, it needs to be carefully attended in the hope that seed from it or another cultivar crossed with it will produce more like it. If the type looks attractive, then it should be described and given a type name drawing attention to its distinguishing characteristics. This will readily identify the type and hopefully preserve it in the future by encouraging growers of seedlings to save only those cultivars which conform closely to type.

Unfortunately, the saving of pretty cultivars which do not embody the standards of type will, within a short period of time, eliminate the original type. Therefore, a special effort should be made to raise cultivars which are true to type.

1 Lifting, Dividing and Storing Tubers

Lifting the Clumps

At the end of their flowering season, dahlia plants show that they have stopped producing new growth. Watering will usually have been curtailed considerably and the plants are maturing along with the tubers they have formed during the flowering season. It is not necessary to wait for the plants to die back as there is little if any sap moving in them. Furthermore, in Australia, most areas will not have a killing frost to cut the plants to soil level. So we can safely cut the tops and lift the clumps of tubers just as is done in other parts of the world where the clumps must be lifted after the first cold snap if they are to be saved.

The stalks may be a little green at this time but this does not matter provided that the tubers are satisfactorily covered in storage. The season's growth should be removed by cutting just above ground level with a pair of secateurs. Make sure that the first ties at the base of the plant are removed as, during the digging of the clumps, these can cause many broken necks which render the tubers useless.

The ideal way to lift the tubers is to use two shovels or spades. To cut the long feeder roots, insert a spade to its full depth around the clump about 30 centimetres from the stake. Then dig each spade into the ground on either side of the clump and push the two handles apart to raise the tubers to the surface, while supporting them from underneath. At this stage the tubers must be handled very carefully in order to avoid neck damage. Leave the adhering soil around them until several clumps have been lifted, then wash them with a jet of water forceful enough to remove the soil but not severe enough to damage any advanced eyes or break the necks of the tubers.

The clumps should be left where they are for an hour or two exposed to the air. This will set the necks and skin on the tubers sufficiently to make the clumps a little more rigid. However, great care is necessary when removing the clumps to adequately support the tubers so that the necks are not bent under their own weight and consequently broken. Once the neck is broken, it is unlikely to allow any

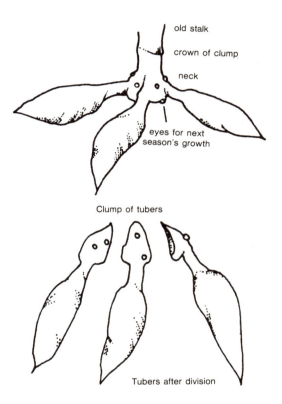

old stalk

crown of clump

neck

eyes for next season's growth

Clump of tubers

Tubers after division

plant food from the tuber to the eyes to promote new growth.

Dividing Clumps

Taking one cultivar at a time, cut each tuber from the main stem with a sharp knife. Each tuber should have an adjoining eye and sufficient stalk should be left around this to support it. Tubers which have long spindly necks should not be moved but divided in the position in which they have been washed off, as their weight may break the joining necks if the clump is raised. Cut surfaces should be dusted with sulphur, and the name of the cultivar should be printed on each tuber with indelible pencil or water resistent marking pen so that it will not lose its identification. Care must be exercised when using sulphur on cut tubers because it will also burn the eyes.

All clumps should be divided and put away under sand, soil or other material on the same day they are dug, to avoid shrinkage. Leaving them out overnight would also bring heavy losses in the event of a frost. Any clumps which have been lifted and cannot be divided and stored should be covered with a plastic sheet, grass or other suitable material to protect them overnight.

Most dahlia growers would be happy to demonstrate their procedure to you. Naturally, you will find that there are many variations to the method described here.

There are also many "old wives tales" which experience has disproved. Some growers still have strong views about leaving dahlias for months to mature before lifting them.

Any stakes which have not been loosened by the digging of the tubers can be removed from the bed by tapping them on the top as if to drive them into the ground. This will release their grip and they can then be removed easily. They should be carefully stored out of the weather for re-use next season.

Storing

The ideal storage place for the tubers is a rack consisting of trays about 75 to 100 mm deep in which the tubers can be laid and covered with damp sand or other material. The rack should be sheltered from the rain and too much sunshine. A shed which is cool and airy is an ideal place for it. When the tubers are first bedded down, the trays should be watered to settle the sand around them, but after this only a light watering need be given about once a month, to keep the tubers plump without forcing growth.

Any unwanted growth which is produced before planting should be left on the tubers, even if they should come into bud or flower, until about a week before planting, when it should be cut back to just above the first node. Fresh strong growth will then begin. If growth is removed several times before planting, weak spindly growth will result. Too much early growth is usually a result of too much moisture, although heat also plays its part.

If you wish to take green plants in the spring, the tubers should be bedded down as described above, in a bench in a glasshouse or glassframe. These tubers will need regular watering in the spring so that they produce fresh growth which can be used for green plants.

Building a Glasshouse

There are a number of different successful approaches to the building of a glasshouse or glassframe in a warm climate. The following points are, however, worth consideration should you wish to construct one for yourself:

• The eastern, northern, and western aspects should be as open as possible to obtain the maximum benefit from the sun's rays in both light and warmth.

• The walls can be constructed of glass or opaque plastic. The glass is whitened to prevent the direct sunlight through the glass from burning the plants.

• The frame to support the sides and roof should be constructed of a material as light as possible to obtain the maximum sunlight in the house.

• If the house is artificially heated, you will be able to take cuttings earlier than if you have to wait for the weather to supply the necessary heat.

• Dahlia cuttings taken in October and early November are ready for planting into beds in late December. These later cuttings do not have extensive root growth in the pot and respond with quick growth after being planted out into the bed.

2 Propagation of Green Plants

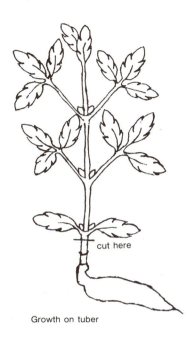

Growth on tuber

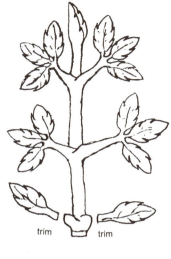

Cutting

Taking the Cutting from the Tuber Growth

In the spring when shoots are about 75 to 100 mm long, cut them with a razor blade just below a node (leaf joint) but be sure to leave at least one node on the remaining section of the shoot attached to the tuber, to ensure the continuance of growth. If other eyes appear around the base of the main shoot, these can be left to grow. It is best to take cuttings in the evening, as the cooler temperature overnight ensures that they do not suffer so severe a set-back.

Planting and Cultivation

The cutting taken from the tuber should be planted about half its length into a bed or pot of perlite, vermiculite, coarse sand or other suitable well draining material, mixed together with peat moss in the proportions of two parts potting medium to one part peat moss. Label the cutting to retain its identity. It must be planted under glass where the air is relatively stationary as this helps to reduce the rate of transpiration in these young plants and provides the necessary humidity and warmth. A glasshouse, glassframe, plastic house or even glass or plastic jars turned upside-down and placed over the plants will suffice.

Water after planting and keep the bed damp so that the plants never suffer from a lack of moisture. In hot weather, frequent washing off reduces the temperature and increases the humidity, which in turn reduces the rate of transpiration and keeps the plants in growing condition. Some water supplies deliver water with a high salt content and a number of other chemicals added. Dahlia plants are very sensitive to these impurities in the water and could die with its use. Rainwater is necessary to save your plants in these circumstances and it should be used on your cuttings while they are in the glasshouse. Once the plants are fully established as green plants in potting soil, they seem to be more tolerant.

Hormone rooting powders or solutions suitable for softwood cuttings can be used. They hasten callousing of the cut end and are purported to promote the growth of roots. However, cuttings of dahlias, given the right conditions, will strike quite readily without using hormones. Regardless of whether hormones are used or not, the cuttings of comparatively harder-wooded dahlia cultivars will take considerably longer than those of softer-wooded cultivars.

Potting

About twenty-one days after planting, some of the cuttings will have made new growth, indicating that roots have formed and that they are ready for potting. The cuttings can be removed easily with a small trowel or similar implement, particularly if a slow stream of water is allowed to run on the bed where the plant is being dug out. 100 to 125 mm pots are ideal for growing on these plants.

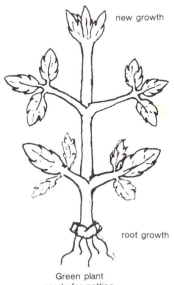

Green plant
ready for potting

The potting medium should be two parts soil containing humus, one part peat moss, and one part sand. A small handful—about 85 gm—of the fertiliser mixture described on page 38 should be added to about 20 L of this potting medium. Prepare a small quantity of this mixture, water it well, and let it stand for about a week before use. It should be used within three weeks. It should be kept moist.

When potted, the plants should be well watered to settle the soil around the roots and to prevent them from drooping. They can now be placed outside in an area protected from wind and excessive sunshine, to harden off and grow on, ready for planting into the main bed. The pots will need watering each morning and if the weather is hot they will also require washing off with a fine spray of water once to three times during the day, according to the temperature.

At least one week, and preferably two or three weeks, should elapse before the plants are put out into the garden bed. About a month after planting they look the same as plants grown from tubers.

Latecuttings

Latecuttings is a single word used to describe the method of preservation of dahlia cultivars by taking cuttings late in the flowering season and growing the mature green plants as stock plants to produce batches of cuttings for green plants for the next flowering season.

It has been known for some time that dahlias growing in the tropical area of northern Australia will continue to grow all year round. To obtain stock after the plants are exhausted from continually growing, fresh tubers are purchased from the south.

Over the last 25 years Swami Vinayananda of New Delhi, India, has developed a method of handling dahlias in the tropical plains area of India. In this area dahlias are mainly grown in flower pots for verandah, rooftop and garden display as well as for exhibition purposes. Both of these aspects of dahlia growing have considerable possibilities for dahlia growers, not only in the tropical north of Australia, but in the southern areas as well, with certain aids to create the climatic conditions required.

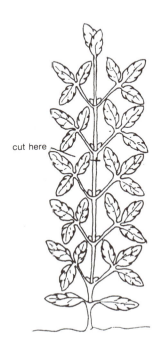

cut here

Top cutting

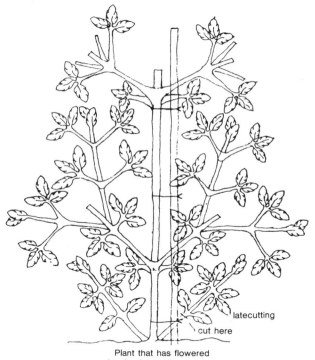

latecutting

cut here

Plant that has flowered
showing latecuttings at base

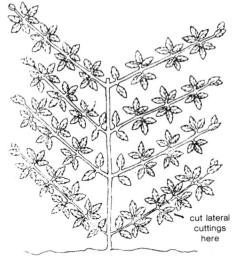

Bud left to flower if required
to identify cultivar

cut lateral
cuttings
here

Stock plant ready to
take lateral cuttings

Swami Vinayananda's method is as follows:

Five green plants, from latecuttings taken late in the flowering season are planted into a potting mixture consisting of either 5 parts of top soil with a tested pH reading of 6.5 (or 3 parts of top soil and 2 parts of decayed leaf mould) and 3 parts of decayed cow or other farmyard manure. That is, if the decayed leaf mould is not available, increase the quantity of top soil used. The top soil should be corrected to pH 6.5, if necessary, before use. The decayed manure and leaf mould would need to be pulverised. Add 85 gm of the fertiliser mixture described on p.38 to approximately 20 L of the potting mixture and stir well every few days. The potting soil should be kept moist all the time. The mixture should be ready for use in about ten days. Prepare sufficient for use in advance of your requirements. It can be used for three or four weeks after it has been prepared.

A 260 mm pot is used for the five green plants. Ensure that the pot has several outlets and provide good drainage at the bottom. Partly fill with the potting mixture; place the five green plants into position then fill the pot to within 20 mm of the top. This will allow room for watering and applying liquid fertiliser, if necessary. However, these plants should not require any more fertiliser nor liquid manure.

Stock plants as they are now called are stopped at 150 mm, about the fourth set of leaves stage. If the plant is over 220 mm high the piece taken from the top to reduce it to 150 mm may be treated as a cutting, hardened off as a green plant, then planted with others to form another stock plant. When the laterals have developed, they are stopped at 100 mm, about the third leaf stage. The same procedure can be followed with these cuttings if they are long enough. If necessary, one lateral growth is allowed to produce a flower as a means of identifying an unnamed plant. Any wrongly named plants can also be checked in a similar manner and corrected. As this stopping is done early, in the rainy or wet season, prior to the need for green plants which will be planted for flowers, these green plants can be added to the stock plants and increase the number of cuttings which can be obtained from the one cultivar for that season. As there would be possibly four leaf joints, or nodes, at the first stopping and about three on the second stopping, and possibly a third stopping, and all cuttings taken thereafter are cut leaving a node at the base of the growth, near the stem, each plant has a potential to produce many cuttings, in batches, for planting for flowers, in the one season.

As the cuttings are young and tender they will root quickly. They strike best in the cooler months in the tropics. The latecuttings are taken from the base of the flowering plants at the end of the flowering season, when the wet season begins. When the roots begin to grow on these cuttings, the young green plants are potted into 130 mm pots and hardened off before being planted into 260 mm or

300 mm pots to be used as stock plants. These stock plants with roots rather than tubers are superior to plants with tubers for taking cuttings because they do not produce flower buds as quickly. Whether potting green plants into 130 mm pots, green plants for stock plants into 260 mm pots or green plants for flower pot dahlias, the same potting mixture as described on page 11 is used.

Green plants from cuttings taken from stock plants are hardened off for up to fourteen days only. The first two days they need to be protected from the full rays of the sun. Gradually, they are exposed to the full sunshine, which they need for about three days before they are planted out into the bed or in flower pots. (See chapter on flower pot dahlias.) Locally, in our Mediterranean climate, green plants are usually commencing to make tubers when they are ready to plant out into the dahlia bed.

Although the latecutting method eliminates the need for tubers after the latecuttings have been taken and established as stock plants, cuttings taken thereafter without trimming to a node are claimed to produce tubers which will grow normally from then onwards. That is, they produce shoots for future growth. However, because of the continuous growing conditions, this may be that the plant does not die back to the tuber as ours do and the new growth is from the first node up the stem.

In India, they are able to send about sixty cuttings in a plastic container with some water in it by the quickest means possible over short distances.

Of course, the tropical climate with a change of the flowering season to the cooler, dry season, and the very hot day and night temperatures in the wet season, all provide a ready made situation for this method to be used.

However, the only reason why the method could not be used in a temperate or cool climate with the aid of artificial light and heat control would be the cost. This cost would have to be compared with the high cost of transporting plants from the tropics to southern Australia. An enclosure protecting the operation from the chilly winter weather would be essential. Heat would be continually needed at the base of the plants and this would need to be thermostatically controlled. Fluorescent or similar lights would provide overhead heat and light at night and a heavy black plastic sheet provided to be drawn as a curtain during the day to turn the day into night and control the length of the daylight hours.

This equipment would enable the grower to control both the temperature at about 24°C and the daylight hours at ten to fourteen hours daily by turning the day into night and the night into day.

It would be an ideal method to use to increase the stock of new or old cultivars in short supply. A few green plants could be carried through the southern winter and used to take the cuttings for green plants for planting in the beds in the late spring.

The author can vouch for the fact that dahlias do not require a dormancy period, having grown tubers imported from the United Kingdom and grown straight on for our season after the end of the Northern Hemisphere season.

Swami Vinayananda has certainly used his enthusiasm for dahlias to the advantage of all dahlia growers. He has been living in an area where it has been possible for him to break away from some of the traditional methods of dahlia growing He has proved that there are many ''old wives tales'', or myths, about dahlia growing that have spread from northern cool and temperate regions.

Species of dahlia grow naturally in the wild untouched areas of the hills in India, similarly to those growing in Mexico. This has given him the opportunity to study them closely. It is most interesting to know that the seasonal reversal for dahlias, from the northern to the southern hemisphere, does not take place at the equator. The change, in low altitude areas anyway, occurs at the tropics where the country is subject to heavy summer rainfall and winter dryness.

The temperatures are warm to hot all year. The daylight hours are always long. The high humidity of the wet season and the more moderate climatic conditions of the dry season make it possible, and, in fact, desirable to treat the wet season as ''winter'' and the dry season as ''summer'' for dahlia growing.

In the northern areas of Western Australia, Northern Territory and Queensland, December to February would be considered to be ''winter'' and June to August ''summer''. These are, of course, opposite to the seasons in the southern temperate and cool regions south of the Tropic of Capricorn.

The latecutting method is an advance upon the mother plant method and offers great potential for commercial dahlia growers who are able to afford the necessary equipment to create climatic conditions, in a glasshouse, similar to those of the tropics. Surely, this is a method awaiting development in Australia.

It would be a tremendous boost to the Australian Dahlia Council to add dahlia societies in the tropical areas of northern Australia to its membership. This would allow an exchange of knowledge on dahlia growing throughout the entire continent. Only India, as far as we know, would be in a position to cover such a wide range of climatic conditions.

Labels

Labels are among the most important items of dahlia culture. A tuber or a green plant without its name is almost useless to a dahlia grower. Without a name or seedling reference, an unnamed plant could be any size and type. It could be a Giant Decorative or a Miniature Cactus, even a Pompon. A friend may have given it to a grower who does not grow these particular types. Furthermore, it will take a full season to find out that it is an unwanted type.

· Therefore, tubers are best labelled with their names printed on them with an indelible pencil or a water resistant wick pen. Tags attached to old stalks after digging the clumps of tubers often break away from the clump to which they refer. While a batch label on a tray or shelf of tubers is helpful to locate particular cultivars, the tubers must also be named. Cuttings should be immediately and consistently named with labels placed in their pots. When they are transferred to other pots to grow on and harden off, labels are again required.

When planting tubers or green plants out into a bed, it is wise to have a plan of the bed with the names or references of the plants marked on it, row by row. Such a plan shows where they are to be planted. This plan can be prepared in advance of planting time, during the winter season. Colours and sizes of flowers and plants can be placed to give a desirable result when they are in bloom. A check can be made of the plants required and any shortages suitably filled either from other sources or with different cultivars of a similar size and type. Labels can be placed on the stakes too to identify the cultivars to any visitors to your garden. However, the master plan is of tremendous value to a dahlia grower and provides a reliable back-up to his bed of dahlias in the event of labels being removed.

White metal labels are considered to be the best. They show themselves conspicuously and are long lasting. Plastic labels are also good but remember that some plastic does break down when exposed to sunshine and the weather. The labels become extremely brittle and break quite easily when they are handled. Visitors can unknowingly cause much concern to the grower merely by handling these brittle labels to identify the cultivars.

Your own unnamed tubers and plants should be tossed among the rubbish and destroyed rather than given to another person to cause them dissatisfaction. Incorrect naming is also a serious problem and care should be taken to correct any known mistakes in names; even incorrectly spelt names cause concern. Cultivars which are passed to other growers incorrectly named often stay that way. The raiser, if available, is the most reliable source of information about the correct name and its spelling.

Cuttings

Green plants

3 Soil Preparation

Dahlias will grow in almost any well-drained soil, but a good crumbly loam, which encourages more extensive root growth, gives the best results. A well-developed root system ensures that plants have greater stamina and better quality flowers.

Drainage

Double digging in autumn–winter will assist drainage in heavy soil:

• Remove the top-soil from the first two or three rows of digging and place it at the other end of the bed.

• Then dig over and break up the sub-soil.

• Place the top-soil from the next two or three rows on top of that sub-soil.

• Repeat this process until the other end of the bed is reached. To complete the bed, cover the last rows of sub-soil with the soil taken from the first two or three rows.

• Avoid bringing the sub-soil to the surface or mixing it with the fertile top layer. If available, compost material can be incorporated with the sub-soil as it is dug over and this will help keep it open.

The benefit of this work will be reaped when heavy rains fall during the early part of the growing season. Having double dug your bed in this manner, it should remain well drained for several seasons. Agricultural pipes may be necessary where soil drainage is very poor.

Planting a Green Crop

Early in winter, June or early July, is the time to plant a green crop of your choice: tick-beans, field peas, mustard, barley, rye-corn, or other suitable crop. It will grow fairly rapidly in the early spring and be ready for turning into the soil at the end of September while the soil is still moist and the crop is lush, but neither rank nor mature. If the soil is deficient in nitrogen, the addition of some animal manure at this stage will be beneficial. It will quickly be assimilated into humus in the soil. At least six weeks should be allowed for this material to decay before planting.

Soil pH Balance

The acidity or alkalinity of soil is measured in what is known as pH readings numbered from one to fourteen. Seven is known as neutral. Most plants require an almost neutral soil. Dahlias require a pH reading of 6.5 which is slightly acid. Unless your soil has a reading of about pH 6.5, certain elements of fertilisers will not become available in a form in which your plants can absorb them.

As soils that have a pH reading below 6.5 are too acid for dahlias, this condition must be corrected by the application of slackened or garden lime. This is best applied after the first rough digging which follows the lifting of the clumps of tubers from the previous season's plantings and allowed to weather into the soil. A reading three or four weeks later will determine the new balance of the soil and whether or not it requires further correction.

On the other hand, soils above pH 6.5 are too alkaline and will also need correcting by the application of agricultural sulphur after the first digging; this is lightly hoed into the top-soil. Again tests after three or four weeks will determine the new balance.

A testing kit developed by the CSIRO is available at some garden supply stores. The directions are easy to follow and a fairly accurate pH reading of the soil can be obtained by this method. Soil can also be tested by using litmus solution or litmus paper. The results are not as informative but do indicate whether the soil is alkaline or acid. Other testing kits are becoming available with additional features including nutrient readings. They are available from some garden centres and are recommended to dahlia gardeners.

Decaying pine bark and other acid compost material such as oak leaves added to the soil will also assist in correcting the pH balance of alkaline soils. Care is also necessary when choosing fertilisers to use. Some supply sulphur or some other acid material. Others have salts which are equivalent to lime.

If there is a high salt content in your soil, heavy waterings will help to wash it through into the sub-soil, away from the roots of your plants. Salt also affects the availability of plant foods.

Final Preparations

- It is advisable to dig the soil finally about a week before planting to bring it to the fine tilth which enables the roots of the dahlia to spread easily.
- In poorer soils, it may be necessary to apply some fertiliser at this stage, particularly if a green crop and animal manures have not been added earlier. The mixture recommended for fertilising on p.38 can be used.
- After the bed has been staked (see p.33) the soil should be watered and left for a day or two before planting takes place.

Large, Ball type

1. 'Risca Miner'

2. 'L'Ancresse'

3. 'Mrs Brown'

4. 'Kent'

5. 'Asana Yama'

Small, Ball type

6. 'Bitsa'

7. 'Alltami Cherry'

8. 'Sea Kiss'

9. 'Red Admiral'

10. 'White Nettie'

17

Pompon type

11. 'Willo Fleck'

12. 'Mark Willo'

13. 'Buttercup'

14. 'Little Snowdrop'

15. 'Pop Willo'

Orchid type

16. 'Koala'

17. 'Pink Orchid'

18 'Seattle Star'

19. Seedling

20. Seedling

Stellar type

21. 'Jescot Lyca'

22. 'Christie Jess'

23. 'Jescot Julie'

24. 'Acacia Julie'

25. 'Pink Giraffe'

Nymphea type

26. 'Figurine'

27. 'Cameo'

28. 'Landis'

29. 'Red Velvet'

30. 'Brunell'

19

Giant, Formal Decorative type

31. 'Edge of Gold'

32. 'Springfield Lavender'

33. 'Louisa Rossack'

Large, Formal Decorative type

34. 'Dad's Day'

35. 'Santa Anita'

Medium, Formal Decorative type

36. 'Maggie Hannaford'

37. 'Alloway Cottage'

38. 'Bob Stanners'

39. 'Formby Lavender'

40. 'Purple Joy'

Small, Formal Decorative type

41. 'Formby Gem'

42. 'George Matherson'

43. 'Alden Blue Hills'

44. 'Pink Frank Hornsey'

45. 'Frank Hornsey'

46. 'Suffolk Hero'

Miniature, Formal Decorative type

47. 'Glacier'

48. 'Eastwin'

49. 'Sally Ann'

50. 'Sandra'

21

Giant, Informal Decorative type

51. 'The Master'

52. 'My Doris'

53. 'Evelyn Rumbold'

54. 'Lena Lila'

55. 'Brenton Sellick'

56. 'Croydon Superior'

Large, Informal Decorative type

57. 'Barbara Elaine'

58. 'Madeline Ann'

59. 'Kidd's Climax'

60. 'Almand's Climax'

Medium, Informal Decorative type

61. 'Formby Supreme'

62. 'Gilt Edge'

63. 'Edna C'

64. 'Mrs A. Woods'

65. 'Gold Coast'

Small, Informal Decorative type

66. 'Jimmy Meredith'

67. 'Ann's Delight'

68. 'Wonder City'

Miniature, Informal Decorative type

69. 'Christie Red'

70. 'Shirley Pride'

23

Giant, Semi-cactus type

71. 'Maxmann'

72. 'St Joan'

73. 'Elmbrook Rebel'

74. 'Gay Triumph'

75. 'Florence Baker'

Large, Semi-cactus type

76. 'Gay Beauty'

77. 'Gay Gertie'

78. 'Candy Keene'

79. 'Reginald Keene'

80. 'Doc. Van Horn'

Medium, Semi-cactus type

81. 'Gay Pride'

82. 'Silver Gay'

83. 'Bob's Gold'

84. 'Lavender Gay'

85. 'Formby Sparkle'

Small, Semi-cactus type

86. 'Gay Delight'

87. 'Gay Lollypop'

88. 'Gay Master'

89. 'Gay's Choice'

90. 'Whiston Sunrise'

25

Miniature, Semi-cactus type

91. 'Elaine Gay'

92. 'Jean'

93. 'Gay Prince'

94. 'Brian's First'

95. 'Match'

Giant, Cactus type

96. 'Pooraka Snowstorm'

97. 'Alden Imperial'

98. 'Alden Joy'

99. 'Griffin's Pride'

100. 'Daleko Jupiter'

Large Cactus type

101. 'Comment'

102 'Golden Planet'

103. 'Gambier Jewel'

104. 'Hamari Katrina'

105. 'Como Tresbon'

Medium, Cactus type

106. 'Jan Lennon'

107. 'Susan French'

108. 'Sunset'

109. 'Daleko Venus'

110. 'Heather'

Small, Cactus type

111. 'Desert Lodge'

112. 'Gay Snowdrop'

113. 'Barbara Kappler'

114. 'Bertie Bromley'

115. 'Sharon Gay'

Miniature, Cactus type

116. 'Grace Candy'

117. 'Debutante'

118. 'Alden Snowlodge'

119. 'Red Regal'

120. 'Milford'

Large, Pincer/Exhibition Cactus type

121. 'Freelancer'

122. 'Cricket'

123. 'Ballerina'

124. 'Gwen's Choice'

125. 'Gloaming'

Large, Fimbriated type

126. 'International'

127. 'Snow-N-Tell'

128. 'Wavabeauta'

129. 'Helen Louise'

130. 'Frontispiece'

Small, Fimbriated type

131. 'Pink Lace'

132. 'Fresco'

133. 'Apache'

Small, Pincer/Exhibition Cactus type

134. 'Jo Jo'

135. 'Town Topic'

Anemone type

136. 'Comet'

137. 'Fabel'

138. 'Grisby'

139. 'Honey'

Collarette type

140. 'Limit'

141. 'Clem's Yellow'

142. 'Bushfire'

143. 'Hades'

Garden display blooms

144. 'Libby's Choice'

145. 'Gambier Princess'

146. 'Maureen Quigley'

147. 'Oriental'

148. 'Bertie Bromley'

149. Giant Decorative

150. Large & Medium Decorative

151. Medium Semi-cactus

152. Large & Medium Cactus

153. Large Fimbriated

154. Medium Semi-cactus

155. Large & Medium Semi-cactus

156. Small Cactus

157. Semi-cactus

158. Small Cactus

159. Miniature Cactus

160. Miniature Decorative

4 Planting

The time for planting dahlias is from spring to New Year's Day. Early plantings are usually made when cut flowers are wanted for selling or house decoration during the summer months of January and February. Later plantings will provide flowers in the autumn when the weather is cooler, particularly at night, and these flowers will be better formed and the colours much brighter. The time for planting also varies with the locality. In Adelaide, for instance, the planting time in the Mount Lofty Ranges is earlier than in the Adelaide Plains. In other States, climatic variation will alter the time of planting. The tropics have different conditions: wet and dry seasons and warm temperatures all year. (See p.11–13.)

Dahlias need a sunny situation sheltered from strong winds, if possible, and receiving some later afternoon shade. They prefer to have an area devoted entirely to them, and not be mixed with other plants.

Staking the Bed

It is best to stake the bed first as this not only indicates where the plants are to be placed, but also eliminates the possibility of root damage. Stakes should be placed 60 cm by 60 cm apart for small-flowered cultivars, and up to 75 cm by 90 cm apart for giant-flowered cultivars.

Place the outside row of stakes all around the bed, measuring out the correct distance each time. Once the outside row is correctly positioned, a string can be tied between these stakes to determine where the inside rows are to be placed. Garden stakes 1.5 m long and 25 mm in width and breadth are those most commonly used. Some taller-growing small and medium sized cultivars may require stakes 1.8 m long.

In addition to the timber garden stakes which are readily available at many hardware and garden stores, stakes can be of other materials, from bamboo canes to lengths of steel reinforcing rod. To add strength to the bamboo canes, fencing wire can be run along the tops of the canes and anchored to a stout stake at both ends of each run.

For larger plantings of dahlias, stakes can be rather expensive. There are alternatives which may be satisfactory and cost less money. A trellis consisting of steel fencing posts, placed about five metres apart with fencing wires threaded through them about 200 mm apart will provide a firm base to which the plants can be tied. Alternatively, an open, thick gauge wire mesh can also be placed between fencing posts to take the place of stakes.

An open mesh net with about 100 mm square openings can be woven out of thick string. Beds of plants in two or three rows can be covered with this net or the wire netting mentioned above, held firmly at the corners and along the sides with stakes. The plants can grow through the mesh which will support them. The mesh can be raised, but taller growing plants could become a problem. Additional lengths of the mesh would be required. The mesh also makes it difficult to cultivate the bed.

One major problem caused by long lengths of wire or netting down the beds is that they create a barrier to anyone wishing to cross the bed, to either attend to the plants or pick the flowers.

Planting Tubers

Tubers with shoots longer than 25 mm should be cut back to just above the first node about a week before planting, and watered so that new growth begins before the time for planting. They should be planted horizontally with the shoot about 25 mm from the stake and 120 mm to 160 mm deep. The soil is cooler at this depth than it is nearer the surface. Tuber and plant losses occur through burning heat at a shallow depth. However, the general rule is for shallower planting in heavy soil, and deeper planting in light soil. After planting, the bed should be given a good watering to settle the soil around the tubers and shoots.

Planting Pot Tubers and Green Plants

Green plant
ready for planting in bed

Pot tubers and green plants should be knocked out of their pots, submerged in a bucket of water, and the soil washed off. The roots can easily be straightened under water, then planted into the soil a little deeper than they were in the pot. To settle the plant into the bed, a slight depression should be made around it so that a thorough soaking can be given; or the plants should be watered thoroughly with a sprinkler, provided that not too much time is allowed between planting and watering.

Early morning and evening are the coolest and best times of the day in which to transplant these plants. If the weather is warm, it may be necessary to place a few sticks on the northern and western sides of the young green plants so as to throw shade over them during the day. A piece of fly wire, bent around each plant in a position where it will provide shade, also helps save the plants from scorching. The danger of scorching is particularly severe with young tender green plants which have not been hardened sufficiently before planting into the bed. It is wiser to leave them in a partly protected area for another week or two as they will soon catch up with the earlier plantings.

If any green plants are left over after planting, leave them in their pots and water them during the growing season. They will make small tubers (pot tubers), which are ideal for planting the next season. Some dahlia cultivars do best when grown from pot tubers. It is also possible to take one or two cuttings from these pot tubers without spoiling them for planting. The tubers should be repotted in fresh potting mixture in the spring and treated similarly to green plants until required for planting into the bed. In some cases the small clumps of tubers can be divided to give two or three plants.

Green plants can also be taken during February and March. Small laterals can be suitably pruned and planted. They will make small swollen roots (pot tubers) which will begin growing again the following spring. If you have a promising new seedling, it is a good idea to take two or three of these autumn cuttings in case the tubers do not keep in storage. Too often new cultivars are lost in the first year's storage.

5 Watering

How Plants Use Water

Plants draw water from the soil with their roots, transport it through trunk or stems, and emit it as vapour from pores in the leaves. This loss of water is called transpiration. While there is sufficient water in the soil for the needs of the plant, the cells remain swollen; that is, the plant is upright and growing, and its leaves are stretched out to the sun.

When the moisture in the soil decreases below a certain level, the plants can no longer draw their requirements from the soil. They close their leaf pores and stop growing. If there is any further decrease in the amount of moisture in the soil, the plants droop and, if water is not applied within a reasonable time, will permanently wilt. It is up to the grower to determine when the plants require further applications of water to keep them in growing condition. Research has established that better crop yields are produced when plants are maintained in growing condition throughout their development.

Water Needs of Dahlias

The best method of watering dahlias is with a fine spray sprinkler set at such a level that it will water the plants overhead until they start to flower, and then over the foliage but below the flowers. Border sprays, lengths of iron or plastic piping with side spray jets spaced at regular intervals, are ideal for this purpose and apply water very evenly to the garden.

The nature of the soil plays a very important part in determining the rate at which you can apply water and the quantity of water to be applied at one time. For instance, sandy soils can absorb water quickly, and therefore a sprinkler with a large opening can be used.

On clay soils, a finer spray should be used, so that it will take longer to apply the same quantity of water, for clay soils do not absorb water as quickly as sandy soils. If sprinklers with large openings are used on clay soil, puddles of water form and pack the top soil down hard, excluding air from the soil, and allowing the water to run off the garden bed. If a single-jet rotary type of sprinkler is used, the area covered is far greater, and so it takes longer to apply the same quantity of water to the soil.

A simple method of gauging the quantity of water applied to the garden is to place cans with straight sides in several positions under the sprinkler, where they will catch only the spray from the sprinkler and not the rebound from plants, fences, or other objects. You will probably find that the quantity of water collected close to the sprinkler is different from that received further away from it. Knowing this, you will be able to overlap the sprinkler watering area so that each part of the bed receives a similar amount of water, and by timing how long the sprinkler has been running and measuring the water in the cans, you will know how long you must leave your sprinkler in one position to apply, say, 25 mm of water to the soil.

However, 25 mm of water applied to sandy soil will penetrate much deeper than the same quantity applied to clay soil. The day after watering, dig a hole in the garden and see how far the water has penetrated after the known period of watering. You can then determine for how long water must be applied to penetrate to the maximum root depth of the plants.

Dahlia plants suffer from lack of water but they also droop if the soil is very wet and the weather very hot; at this stage, a wash-off of the foliage with a fine spray of water will restore them to the erect state. But when they droop four or five days after watering, although the temperature is not very warm, it indicates that a further watering to root depth is required; a wash-off will temporarily restore them. Dahlia plants, particularly tuber plantings, should not be overwatered in the early stages of growth. The soil should never be waterlogged because the fine hair-like feeder roots will rot and the whole plant collapse. This is why good drainage is essential.

In the absence of sufficient rainfall, once a week watering in the first six to eight weeks of growth is recommended to give the young plants a good start.

At about the eighth week after planting, plants should be well developed, and as with any large plant having many leaves, the rate of transpiration of water during hot weather and low humidity will be very high. Mulching, and fine sprays on hot days, will help retain the moisture in the soil and prevent plants from drooping. A mulch will also reduce the variation in the temperature of the soil between day and night and in the event of sudden cold weather.

However, watering should continue about every four days, depending upon your soil's ability to retain sufficient water to maintain it in a fairly moist condition. A simple test is to obtain a handful of soil out of a shallow hole and press it together: if it remains in a ball, it is satisfactory; if it crumbles, it requires more water.

Waterings penetrating to the root depth of the plants and heavy enough to saturate the soil are best applied in the mornings when the soil will warm up quickly during the day. If applied in the evening, heavy watering will chill the soil, delaying growth early in the season, and later in the season causing the flowers to throw open their centres. Of course, eventually, the cold nights will do this anyway, but there is no need to hurry the close of the season. Double flowers will also open their centres quickly under conditions that are too dry.

Dahlia plants do not burn if water is applied to the foliage while the sun is shining on them; in fact, a light spray of water overhead during and after a very hot day is most beneficial to them, as it reduces the rate of transpiration. The water applied must be just enough to dampen the foliage and soil surface. It cannot therefore be considered a watering as it does not penetrate the soil to the roots of the plants.

In some areas certain minerals and chemicals have been added to the water supply for health reasons; also some water has a high concentration of salt in it. Dahlia plants *will* burn if this water is sprayed over them during the heat of the day, the chemicals covering the foliage and causing the burning. Usually watering before the sun is high enough to heat the plants in the mornings and from sunset onwards in the evenings, will overcome this problem. However, if it does not prevent burning, the plants should be trench watered or soaked with water from outlets in piping arranged so that the water does not reach the leaves. Because dahlias like their foliage sprayed with water especially in hot weather, every attempt should be made to do so. Washing the plants with water regularly also reduces the likelihood of an outbreak of red spider and other insects amongst your plants. Rain water or good quality bore water may be available and preferable in extreme circumstances.

6 Weed Control

Weeds should not be allowed to grow among the dahlia plants, as they rob the soil of food and moisture and compete with the plants for light if allowed to grow unchecked. In the early stages of their growth, a light hoeing of the soil the day after watering will keep them under control. Do not hoe too deeply as this will break the roots of the dahlia plants. The breaking of the top of the soil allows air and water to enter it more readily. A mulch will also help keep weeds in check.

If a mulch is applied to your dahlia patch early after planting, it should be stirred and the top of the soil under it broken once a fortnight.

All hoeing should cease when the first buds appear on your plants about six weeks after planting. When the plants begin to form buds their fine feeder roots are present in the top soil searching for nutrients, and should not be disturbed. The bushes are well established and will themselves reduce weed growth.

There are, of course, a number of chemical weedicides which could be used to kill off the weeds, but the dahlia plants need the aeration of the top soil. Furthermore, residues of these chemicals could become a problem, and some of the spray on the plants disasterous.

7 Feeding the Soil to Supply Plant Nutrients

The Basic Fertilisers

The three basic fertilisers to be used for dahlias are the same as for other plants—nitrogen, phosphorus, and potash.

Nitrogen produces heavy growth, good foliage, delays flowering, and adds colour and size to flowers if given when the buds are developing.

Phosphorus promotes root growth, ripens plant tissues and seeds, and hastens flowering.

Potash provides starch for tuberous roots, strengthens stems, and adds colour and size to flowers.

When using fertilisers it is important to maintain a balance between the elements you are applying, otherwise you may lose much of their value to the plants. For instance, if you apply a high proportion of nitrogen without sufficient potash, you will have large bushes with plenty of lush foliage but few flowers, weak stems, and limp florets of flowers. Phosphorus is deficient in many Australian soils and can be used, in the correct proportion, on dahlias to their advantage.

The nature of the soil plays an important role in determining the quantities of fertilisers to be used. Sandy soils require more potash than clay soils. Soils which have had farmyard manures applied for a previous crop, or had them and/or a green crop turned into the soil, will require smaller quantities of fertiliser during the growing period. These latter soils will have much plant food available for early growth and possibly will need no further supplies until buds appear.

Fertiliser Proportions for Dahlias

A general mixture which has proved to be satisfactory for dahlias in various districts is:

Volume	Fertiliser
15 kg	nitrogen, low %, e.g. organic nitrogen
9 kg	superphosphate
6 kg	sulphate of potash

Add to ten litres of the above mixture:
400 gm epsom salts (magnesium sulphate)
 85 gm iron sulphate
 85 gm copper sulphate

Alternatively to the above, a 5–10–5 ready mixed fertiliser can be used.

Note:
Other trace elements are required in minute quantities only and it is difficult to spread them evenly in a dry mixture. As a spray, they can be spread more readily. They are usually present in most soils in sufficient quantities and should be used only when deficiencies are indicated by the condition of your plants. Some foliage spray fertilisers contain trace elements to complete the food supplied through the foliage.

If you use a fertiliser which has a higher percentage of nitrogen than has been suggested, then you must increase the superphosphate and sulphate of potash proportionately to maintain the balance. If fertilisers containing a high percentage of nitrogen are used on dahlia beds, the keeping qualities of the tubers will be affected. The more nitrogen you use the more likely it is that the tubers will rot in storage, because of the plant tissues breaking down. This applies equally to the use of farmyard manures in large quantities.

Application of Fertilisers

Fertiliser is best applied little and often rather than in large quantities at one time, as plants can absorb only small quantities of nutrient with the water they draw in through their fine root hairs. If you have applied fertiliser before planting your dahlias, they will not require any more until they reach six to eight weeks of growth. Then the mixture mentioned above can be applied at the rate of a small handful (85 gm) per square metre between the rows, about 20 cm from the stalk. The soil should be moist before the fertiliser is applied, to prevent it from burning the fine roots of the plant. Follow the application of fertiliser immediately with a good watering. It takes approximately three weeks for the plants to show the results of the application of these fertilisers. A further application can be given if it is needed after four or five weeks.

In addition to applying the above fertiliser mixture when the buds appear, a drum of liquid manure can also be prepared. A sack with either pigeon, fowl, sheep or cow manure can be suspended in a drum filled with water for about two weeks. Superphosphate and sulphate of potash should be added to the manure in the sack. The resulting liquid should be diluted by adding one part to 20 parts of fresh water, then watered around the plants, after regular waterings, weekly. Again, caution must be exercised in the quantities used in the preparation and in the use of this liquid manure. The tubers of the plants fed with this liquid will probably fail to store for the next season's planting.

As an alternative to this laborious task of preparing and distributing the liquid manure, a dressing at the rate of 85 gm per square metre of equal parts of sulphate of potash and superphosphate can be applied, then a mulch of cow, sheep or horse manure can be spread sparingly between the rows. The soil should be damp before applying the fertiliser and the mulch. After it has been spread, the bed should again be thoroughly watered.

Another alternative is the use of a complete liquid fertiliser such as Top Soluable, Phostrogen, Aquasol, Thrive or other brands as foliage spray. These fertilisers are quicker acting and can be sprayed on the foliage in the cool of the evening. You should choose the fertiliser that best suits your needs, using the analysis shown on the packets to guide you. The directions on the packet regarding the use of the fertiliser should be followed strictly but erring towards the ''little-and-often'' approach. Excessive use will seriously affect the keeping quality of the tubers. The results of your spraying will be noticeable within about a week.

If your present method of fertilising is achieving good results, be reluctant to change it. If you think better results may be obtained by varying your mixture, experiment, bearing in mind the purpose for which each ingredient is used. Apply varied mixtures to a few plants and keep a record of the mixtures used and the results. This will help you in future seasons.

Soil and the fertilising of it is a very extensive subject, far too great to include in detail in this book. There have been many books published on the subject, so it is recommended that, if you wish to know more about it, you should pursue further reading.

The following list of plant food deficiency symptoms should help you in determining the cause of any poor growth in your dahlias. However, if in doubt, you should consult your local department of agriculture or other authority.

Plant Food Deficiencies

Symptoms appear first in the *oldest* leaves.

Nitrogen	general yellowing; stunting, premature maturity.
Magnesium	patch yellowing; brilliant colours especially around edge.
Potassium	scorched margins, spots surrounded by pale zones.
Phosphorus	yellowing; erect habit; lack-lustre look; blue-green; purple colours.
Molybdenum	mottling over whole leaf but little pigmentation; cupping of leaves and distortion of stems.
Cobalt	legumes only, as for nitrogen.
Excess salt	marginal scorching, generally no spotting.

Symptoms appear first in either the *oldest* or *youngest* leaves.

Manganese	interveinal yellowing; veins pale green, diffuse; water-soaked spots; worst in dull weather.

Symptoms appear first in the *youngest* leaves.

Calcium	tiphooking, blackening and death.
Sulphur	yellowing; smallness; rolled down; some pigmentation.
Iron	interveinal yellowing; veins sharply green, youngest leaves almost white if severe.
Copper	dark blue-green; curling; twisting; death of tips.
Zinc	smallness; bunching; yellow-white mottling.
Boron	margins chlorotic; crumpling; blackening; distortion.

8 Pruning

pinch out

Stopping a plant

It is not essential for the smaller-flowered types of dahlia to be pruned at all, but the shape of the bushes and the quality of the blooms can be improved with a little effort. With the larger-flowered types pruning is necessary to make room for the flowers and increase their size.

Pruning to Induce New Growth

Pruning is also used to induce new, strong, quick growth. When you plant your dahlias, some of the green plants may have very hard or spindly stalks; some tubers will develop more quickly than normal; or you may realise that your plants are too advanced to produce the first flush of blooms for a particular show. These variations from what you require can be corrected in four stages.

1. Pinch out the centre of the plant and allow the side shoots to start growing. This pruning is usually done in the first week in January to be in time for March shows. The cultivar planted, however, plays an important part in determining the time for pruning because soft-wooded cultivars grow more quickly than hard-wooded ones. This is where experience in growing particular cultivars counts in obtaining the flowers when they are required. Generally soft-wooded cultivars grow with longer distances between the nodes than the hard-wooded cultivars, which have only short distances between the nodes. Whether the growth is compact and hard in appearance, or flowing and soft, also helps to determine whether the cultivar is hard- or soft-wooded.

2. Remove the side shoots from the leaf joints, allowing the old stalk and leaves to remain for the time being. Play safe at this stage of pruning by leaving the last pair of shoots above ground level on the plant, until you see the fresh shoots coming through the ground. If these do not appear you can develop a plant from the two shoots that you have left. The growth which comes from the base of the plant will be strong because it has an established root system to support it. It will also grow quickly

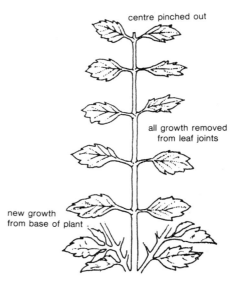

centre pinched out

all growth removed from leaf joints

new growth from base of plant

Pruning to induce new growth from the base of the plant

because the season is right: the ground is warm and the daylight hours are shortening. The reason for leaving the old stem and its leaves after pruning is to obtain the strongest possible watershoots or lateral growths. The development of the old plant has been stopped by removal of all the growing points, but its leaves are essential to promote robust new growth and eventually produce better flowers. The old stem will die when the new growth takes over the plant.

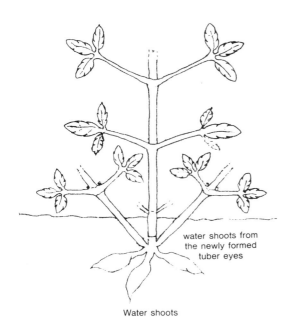

water shoots from the newly formed tuber eyes

Water shoots

Pruned for water shoots

3. The lateral growths and/or watershoots must be restricted to the number required to give you as many flowers of the desired size as the cultivar is capable of producing. Small flowered cultivars can carry many more blooms than large flowered ones. Some cultivars, particularly those in the Giant and Large size groups, can carry more flowers of their full size limit than others without rigorous pruning. These cultivars do not need to be pruned to less than four or five growths from the bottom of the plant. The other cultivars, not capable of producing as many large flowers, need heavier pruning, possibly to only one or two shoots.

It may be necessary to dig around the plant to enable you to do this heavy pruning. Care is needed so as not to disturb the root growth of the plant and cause it to suffer undue stress.

4. When the fresh growth is about 15 cm high, tie the new plant to the stake. As the old stalk has no growing points other than those you have chosen, it can be left on the plant without any ill effect.

Pruning to Shape the Bushes

Having used the method described above to obtain your plant, you will have two or four main stems growing and you will allow the central buds to develop, and prune for size as described later (see p. 42).

Some of your plants will have been just as you wanted them early in January, particularly tuber plantings and giant-flowered cultivars on which it is necessary to grow to one central stalk crown bud, and you will not have had to carry out the above operations. To shape these plants, there are two main approaches:

1. Where a quantity of smaller flowers is required, the centre should be pinched out of the plant when it is about 23 cm high. This will force the side or lateral growths to develop. As they grow you must securely and carefully tie them to the stake to prevent wind damage to the plant, for, when grown, these side laterials very easily break away from the main stem under their own weight.

2. Where larger flowers are required, you will need to limit the number of side growths allowed to develop. This is done by pruning out alternate laterals. If still further pruning is necessary, you can leave only one lateral near the top of the plant, one about halfway down, and allow a further shoot to develop at the bottom of the plant. Remember, the more laterals you allow to grow, the smaller your

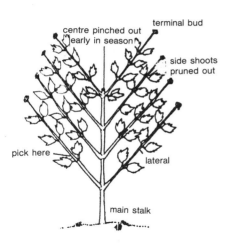

centre pinched out early in season

terminal bud

side shoots pruned out

pick here

lateral

main stalk

After pruning to shape the bush (for small-flowered cultivars)

flowers will be on the Medium, Large and Giant-flowered cultivars.

It is important to do this pruning as soon as you can so that you are not slicing large pieces of lateral growth off your plants; keep the vigour and energy of the plant in the growth you require.

Another important point to remember is that laterals near the top of the plant will flower before those from the bottom of the bush. This does not invalidate the earlier described method of inducing new growth by removing higher side shoots, as the reason for pruning is different. In this case you are allowing top growth to develop which will check the bottom growth.

Pruning to Increase Size of Flowers

With Giant, Large, Medium and Small sized flowers, other than Ball, Pompon, Orchid, Stellar, Anemone and Miniature sized flowers in the Formal Decorative, Informal Decorative, Semi-cactus and Cactus types, it is essential to disbud and prune to obtain full sized blooms. This pruning should be done as early as possible so that the strength of the plant is directed where it is required and not wasted in foliage which will be discarded later. With Giant and Large flowered cultivars which are grown to a plant with one main stalk, a secondary pruning of the plant is made about the time when the bud appears at the top of the plant. This bud is called a **crown bud** to distinguish it

from the buds at the top of the lateral growths which are called **terminal buds**.

Timing the flowers to be at their best on show days is important with these plants because relatively few flowers are allowed to develop in order to obtain the maximum size possible. It is necessary to examine each plant closely to determine which buds and side shoots are to be retained for flowers. A certain amount of knowledge of the growth habits of each cultivar will assist considerably in this decision.

If it is decided to retain the crown bud, and possibly a side bud next to it to obtain extra length of stem or to replace a damaged or mis-shapen bud, the other buds are removed. Then go down the plant removing all unwanted side shoots from the leaf joints, except the three or four chosen to provide flowers later. Remember side shoots near the top of the plant will bloom before those lower down. By saving one near the top, another about half way and others near the bottom of the plant, the flowers will be spread over a period of time. Of course, it is necessary to remove the side shoots from the top of the plant which will be cut with the flower when picked. Choose the stronger growing side shoots if possible. They should not be disturbed at this stage but watched and securely tied as they grow to avoid possible accident or wind damage.

Plants consisting of lateral growths with terminal buds, are treated in a different manner. After removing the surplus buds, the side shoots are removed from all but the last leaf joint on the lateral growth near the main stalk of the plant.

During pruning, any unwanted leaves, especially those likely to damage the flower, should be removed from the plant.

Miniature Sized Flowers

The attractiveness of a Miniature sized flower is in its neat and dainty appearance rather than its size. It is possible to prune a cultivar in this category and obtain flowers larger than the size limit for Miniatures but usually they do not compare favourably with full size flowers of Smalls.

Having shaped the bushes by pinching the centre of the plant earlier in the season, there should be a number of lateral shoots to produce flowers. Miniatures should not be disbudded until the colour of the florets is showing. Then remove only the surplus buds, for it is not usually necessary to prune the side shoots out of the leaf joints on these cultivars. Work carefully so that the pruning is not apparent when the flowers are picked. The appearance of short pieces of side growth left on the stem is very distracting.

The back florets of Ball and Pompon type dahlias should reflex to the stem. To obtain well formed ball-shaped blooms, it is advisable to carefully remove the calyx or outer covering of the bud as part of the disbudding procedure. This can improve the shape and appearance of blooms of these types considerably, especially with those cultivars which have an unusually large calyx.

Picking the Flowers

The flowers should be picked as they develop to maturity unless they are needed to produce seed later in the season. Dead flowers left on the plants will retard future growth. They will also encourage fungal diseases in the patch.

The stems should be cut just above a leaf joint from which future growth will develop. Pieces of stem left above this leaf joint will retard the development of other flowers. While future flowers must be considered when cutting, all flowers should be picked with reasonably long stems. If the growth on top of the bush is rather dense and full of buds, cutting a few flowers with reasonably long stems will allow others more space to develop. This harder pruning and sacrifice of a few buds will be rewarded with new growth to provide more buds for later flowering. It also tends to bring the flowers above the foliage.

Correcting the Angle of the Flower

On some cultivars, the buds may be flat on top of the stem, or at an angle of 90 degrees, instead of being in the ideal position of 45 degrees to the stem. This can be altered with the aid of a "neck stretcher", a piece of heavy gauge wire about 45 cm long, bent to form a crook on the top at the angle to the stem at which the flower is required to grow. At the lower end of the wire loops are made to take rubber bands. The rubber bands are stretched between a loop and a suitable leaf joint to apply a reasonable amount of pressure behind the bud. If the correct pressure is applied, the bud will grow at

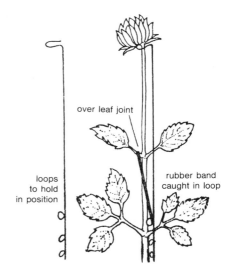

over leaf joint

loops to hold in position

rubber band caught in loop

The neck stretcher

the desired angle to the stem, but too much pressure will nip the bud off, while too little will not correct the angle. It is necessary to examine the bud as it fills out to ensure that the wire is doing its job. The wire is placed in position about two weeks before the flower matures and should not be removed until the bloom is picked.

Buds on large-flowered cultivars must be placed in a position which will enable the bloom to develop evenly. If one half of the flower is higher than the other, the flower often develops more on the lower portion, forming what is called a "beard".

If you have grown a weak-stemmed cultivar, a serious fault in dahlias because this feature has mainly been bred out of them, it is advisable to pick the flower stem at about the same length as, or 25 mm shorter than, the wire, so that during carriage to the show the bloom will be supported by the wire and not the stem. The wire must be removed when the bloom is staged.

Another method of correcting the angle of the flower is to use two pieces of bamboo cane. The two pieces are the two halves of a cane cut lengthwise. They have a hollow centre and any leaf joints in the cane with the centre filled in can be scooped out. They can be fastened around the stem with pegs or pieces of wire twisted to tighten them against the stem. Continuous examination of the stems and buds with suitable adjustment of the canes will gradually place the developing bud in the desired position.

General Observations

• Before pruning a plant, it is a good idea to examine the bush carefully to ensure that you retain the stronger growth. When you select a bud for a flower, be sure it is not mis-shapen or damaged in any way.

• Be sure to remove all shoots cleanly from leaf joints when pruning or further growth may start from the pieces left and the value of pruning will be lost.

• After dahlias have been watered, the plants are very brittle and it is necessary to take care when working among them, otherwise buds or shoots required for flowers may be accidentally broken.

• It is advisable to grow three or four plants of each cultivar. This enables you to spread your buds over the period when show blooms are required. It is also best to grow a few more cultivars than are required. For instance, if you wish to exhibit six distinct cultivars, you should grow at least nine cultivars to increase the possibility of obtaining flowers when needed and provide spare blooms to carry to the show.

• Timing of dahlia flowers for a show is a difficult job because soil, cultivation, and climate can all influence the time a plant will take to flower. It is not possible to lay down hard-and-fast rules on this point, as every person grows the plants a little differently, and soils and temperatures vary within short distances. Hard-wooded cultivars take two or three weeks longer than soft-wooded cultivars to develop their flowers from the small-bud stage. Only a general guide can be given and to this must be added your own experience, in order to produce the desired results. Generally, lateral growth on soft-wooded cultivars will take about six weeks to flower from a shoot 25 mm long. Buds about the size of a pea will take about three weeks to mature.

9 Tying

Dahlia plants are soft and brittle and need to be tied to a stake with coarse string or similar material, to protect them against strong wind and to prevent the bushes from sprawling over the ground. Later in the season, lateral growth will need to be supported in the same manner, to prevent breakage when the gardener is attending to the plants.

After the first tie, when the plants are 15 to 23 cm high, it will be noticed that they make quick progress. In fact any plants which are not growing as quickly as the rest can be encouraged by tying them to the stake. On most bushes, three or more ties are necessary to keep the plants erect.

As the plant grows, some of the early ties may become tight around the stalk. It is advisable to cut these and rely upon the ties higher on the bush to support the plant, as any restriction may interfere with the future growth of plant and blooms.

When placing shades over individual buds, it will be necessary to make additional ties to secure the bud in the centre of the shade. This is done to prevent the flower, when it opens, from rubbing against the shade.

If a stake should be broken in a wind-storm or a bush badly blown about, replace the stake and retie immediately to enable the plant to recover. A plant left in a horizontal position, even for a day, will have the top growth twisted to a vertical position. once this has happened, it is difficult to regain straight stems on the flowers.

10 Shading

The fresh dewy nights and sunny days of autumn provide the best conditions for the development of well-formed dahlia flowers, especially the revolute (rolled or folded) florets of the Cactus type, but sunlight tends to bleach the colour from the back florets before the flower is fully matured. Consequently, the blooms should be shaded if they are to be presented at their best on the show bench. Some cultivars also improve in form when shaded.

Shades should be placed over the buds about one week before the flower matures. Usually the buds are showing the colour of the first row or two of opening florets when the cover is placed over them. A few cultivars will not tolerate shade covers. These need to be grown in a position with natural shade in the afternoons.

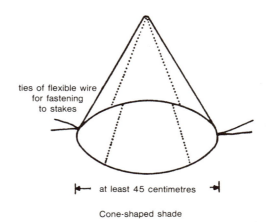

ties of flexible wire
for fastening
to stakes

at least 45 centimetres

Cone-shaped shade

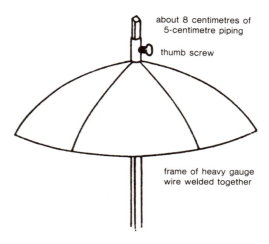

about 8 centimetres of
5-centimetre piping

thumb screw

frame of heavy gauge
wire welded together

Adjustable shade

Making the Shades

Cone-shaped shades which fit inside one another when stored can be made from a framework of fairly heavy gauge galvanised wire or light steel either turned, soldered, or welded together at the joints. The cloth for the shade can be hessian, salon, mutton cloth or stockingette which, in a warm climate, will allow a certain amount of air to circulate inside the shade. In cooler districts, calico or canvas can be used. The open-weave material coverings should be covered with plastic during rain showers, to prevent the blooms from filling with water, which would make them too heavy for the stems to hold without bending or even snapping.

Positioning the Shades

There are two methods of attaching shades to stakes:

1. Three or four points of the shade can be attached to stakes on either side of the bloom to hold it fast even in a fairly strong wind-storm. Light-gauge pliable wire is quite satisfactory and reusable.

2. The frames are made with a piece of piping attached in the centre with a thumb screw screwed into it. This screw can be tightened against the stake to hold the shade firmly.

The bud should be so shaded that when the flower opens fully it will not rub against the shade and become bruised or grow out of shape. It may be necessary to tie the bud in the required position.

The use of 50% nylon shade cloth to protect the plants and blooms from excessive heat is gaining popularity. There are several different approaches to the method of covering:

1. A tubular frame is constructed with a height of three metres. The flat top should be made of suitably spaced lengths of tubing. In between, wires

are used as additional supports to prevent the cloth from sagging. The cloth is placed over the top of the frame only, in a permanent position. Further wires are run across the top of the shade cloth to prevent it from flapping and tearing in the wind. The shade cloth encourages the plants to grow taller than when uncovered. An additional cover is required to protect larger blooms. There is a reduction in the number of flowers produced under shade cloth.

2. Using a similar three metre high frame, the 50% shade cloth is placed on top in a roll at one end. On hot days and when the shows are being held, the shade cloth is unrolled to cover the plants. The plants are almost unaffected by this method.

3. A compromise between the former two methods is to construct a frame with a little sturdier tubing or water pipe. The top instead of being flat is at an angle of 22 degrees, raised on the eastern side of the frame, which is two metres wide. Wire is also used to support the 50% shade cloth which is placed permanently across the top. The plants are in the sun until approximately mid-day, then shaded during the hotter afternoon. The plants are more normal. However, shades are still required for larger blooms for show purposes.

With all the sides open, the air is allowed to circulate freely under these shade cloth covers. The florets of the blooms appear to be more openly spaced and of less substance if the covering is permanent.

Shading the blooms is only essential for exhibitors at shows. Uncovered plants merely means the flowers, particularly the larger ones, will be bleached according to the weather conditions when they are opening. Some colours bleach worse than others.

Umbrellas can also be used as shades for the flowers. The handle is fastened securely to a stake.

11 Flower Pot Dahlias

Some dahlia growers in Australia have shown an interest in growing dahlias in pots but, so far, they have had limited success. Consequently, the plants in bloom have not aroused the enthusiasm necessary to encourage others to follow their lead.

In the tropical plains area of India, a method of growing dahlias in pots has been in use for over fifty years, and is a great and widespread success. These dahlias are used for garden display, verandah and rooftop decoration, and for exhibition, even by beginning growers.

In India flowerpot dahlias are most popular
(*Photo:* Swami Vinayananda)

There is one point on which we are over-cautious when growing dahlias in flower pots: we use limited quantities of fertiliser or manures in order to save our tubers for the following season. The method which has been developed in India uses latecuttings for stock plants to carry over into the next season, eliminating the need to save tubers at all. Consequently, free use of liquid manure and booster fertiliser feeds is not a problem. Apparently with the constant feeding throughout the life of the plant, excellent results can be achieved even by new dahlia growers. Of course, as with any dahlia growing, the plants respond very favourably to careful attention.

All types and sizes of dahlias can be grown successfully in pots. The resultant pot plants, when exhibited in bloom, would certainly give a good indication of the grower's ability to grow the plant and produce the best flowers. At the same time, blooms can be cut from other plants and exhibited as individual specimen blooms of the various sizes and types. Similar remarks apply to garden display cultivars which could also be exhibited as plants or cut blooms arranged in vases or other containers. Apart from the transport difficulties involved, what an impact good flower pot dahlias would have on the general public at our shows. Flower pot dahlias have the advantage of mobility if seed is required. The plants required as parents could be removed to an enclosure to protect them from bees and adverse weather conditions.

Giant and Large Size Cultivars

When these plants are grown in flower pots, they are grown to one flower which is from the crown bud. Side or lateral buds are not used as they would spoil the balance of the plant and would be penalised accordingly. It is difficult to time these blooms to be at their best on the day of the show. In addition to the normal time of about 85 to 100 days for plants to produce blooms, individual cultivars have their own variations which experience alone can teach. Even then abnormal weather conditions during the growing period will have some effect upon the actual time when the bloom will reach its ultimate beauty.

Cuttings of a cultivar taken at the same time will usually flower at the same time, regardless of whether they are transplanted at the same time or not. Therefore, to spread the time of flowering over a few weeks around show time, cuttings taken over a few weeks or more are developed as green plants for planting in pots. Care of the plants from the cutting stage through to flowering is most important. Any set back will be reflected in the quality of the bloom produced.

Medium and Small Size Cultivars

These are grown along the same lines as when grown in garden beds. The plants are stopped at about the fourth set of leaves stage by pinching out the central growing tip of the plant. The laterals are then allowed to develop. They are supported by a separate stake for each to keep it straight and in the position required to produce a well balanced plant. One flower only is allowed to develop on each of these lateral growths. All other side shoots from the leaf joints, except those at the last leaf joint near the central stalk which are left for later flowering, are taken off the plant as soon as they are big enough to remove. This early pruning retains all the plant's energy in the flower being formed from the terminal bud of each lateral.

Miniature and Other Very Small Size Cultivars

These are stopped firstly by pinching out the central growing tip of the plant at the fourth pair of leaves stage. Secondly, each of the laterals is stopped again at the third pair of leaves stage. This then produces a compact plant with many laterals producing a mass of blooms at the same time.

Care must be taken during the whole pruning operation to ensure that the symmetry of the bush is not spoilt.

The only disbudding for these miniature flowers is the removal of the two side buds to allow the terminal buds to flower. When the blooms are picked they are cut with long stems leaving only the last leaf joint near the adjoining stem to develop more laterals for later flowers.

Cultivation of Flower Pot Dahlias

Cuttings are developed as green plants, once they have rooted, by transplanting them into 130 mm pots using the potting mixture mentioned on page 11. The green plants are protected from full sunshine for about three days, and are then gradually exposed to it, reaching full sunshine by the tenth day. After three or four days in the sun they are ready for planting into 260 mm or 300 mm pots.

Good drainage in the pots is absolutely essential. A pot with a number of outlets at the bottom is preferable to a pot with just one hole. Crocks or similar drainage material such as pieces of plastic foam etc. should cover the bottom of the pot.

The pot is half filled with potting mixture. A green plant is then transplanted with the soil intact around its roots. The plant is centrally placed in the larger pot and staked. During the growth of the plant it should be tied securely to the stake with soft string to keep it erect. The pot is then filled to within 20 mm of the top with the potting mixture which is firmed around the plant.

Lateral growths on Medium and Small size cultivars should be supported with additional stakes to keep them straight and well positioned to give a balanced plant.

A small quantity of fresh cow or other farmyard manure is placed in a drum of water to decompose for about fourteen days. The liquid manure is then diluted, one part in twenty parts of clear water. Half a litre of this diluted liquid manure is then given to each flower pot dahlia once or twice a week commencing on the tenth day after the application of the booster feed given fifteen days after transplantation into the larger pot. Liquid manure should only be given after the normal watering, while the soil is moist. Another booster feed is given to the plants when the first bud begins to form. A break of seven days is then taken before the next liquid manure feed. These liquid manure feeds are then continued until the buds show colour.

A booster feed is an application of about 40 gm per plant of the fertiliser mixture mentioned on page 38. This should be placed in a circle around the inside edge of the pot and lightly scratched into the top 20 mm of the soil. All fertiliser should only be applied to moist soil and then watered copiously for three consecutive days after its application.

The usual disbudding is necessary on flower pot dahlias to obtain blooms of full size and good quality. Remember that the crown bud only is kept to develop a flower on Giant and Large size cultivars and the terminal bud of each lateral on Medium and Small size cultivars.

When shoots begin to grow from near the base of flower pot dahlias towards the end of the flowering season, they can be taken as latecuttings and the green plants from them planted as stock plants. Cuttings for the coming flowering season can be taken from these stock plants and any others you may have when the season for taking them commences.

12 Growing Dahlias by the Soilless Method

Dahlias can be grown by the soilless method if you wish. Pots should be 200 mm or larger. Tubs or troughs can also be used. A potting medium such as perlite is necessary to hold the roots and moisture. Green plants are ideal for planting in these soilless pots.

While dahlias are sun-loving plants, under these growing conditions some protection from the direct afternoon sunshine is advisable. They should not be grown under, but on the eastern side of trees where they can receive the morning sunshine.

Watering is required frequently because the drainage must be very efficient. During warm to hot days, two or three thorough waterings are necessary. The plants should not be placed under stress at any time for the want of water.

There are no plant nutrients in the potting medium, these have to be supplied entirely by artificial fertiliser. One of the foliage feed fertilisers would be most suitable for this purpose. You should not consider saving the tubers produced by these plants because they would not store well. Therefore, a complete foliage feed fertiliser such as Top Soluable, Thrive, Aquasol, Urea Plus or Phostrogen would be satisfactory. A fertiliser containing the micro nutrients or trace elements is to be preferred. If the little and often principle of fertilising is adopted, the complete liquid fertiliser may be reduced to about one-third of the strength recommended and used continuously in the normal waterings. One or two heavy waterings fortnightly without any fertiliser should clear any residues from the pot.

Other cultival requirements such as staking, tying, stopping, and disbudding are required as for flower pot dahlias. This method is awaiting further development. It could be used to avoid some of the fungus diseases which are present in the soil. Late-cuttings could be taken from the plants after flowering to provide stock plants for the next season.

13 Selection of Seed Parents

There are a number of important factors to be considered when selecting parent cultivars.

1. **Quality of Tubers** Some cultivars have tubers with undesirable long, thin necks which break easily when being lifted and handled in storage. Others have poor keeping qualities. They have either weak constitutions or they fail to store sufficient plant food in the tubers to maintain the early growth for next season. Good keeping, well formed, medium sized tubers are required.

2. **Satisfactory Bush Growth** Some cultivars grow very lanky, sprawl in spite of ties or lack strength. Weak and crooked stems are to be avoided as an undesirable characteristic of the dahlia which has mainly been bred out of cultivars by suitable culling. Breeders should ensure that seedlings with weak or crooked stems are destroyed regardless of the quality of the bloom as their presence in the garden is very likely to affect future seedlings.

A relatively compact bush of firm substance, good foliage and reasonably long, strong and straight stems with pairs of leaves placed to suit the flowers it carries, are growth habits to strive for.

3. **True to Form Flowers** It is fairly well known that top ranking cultivars, consistent with the standard form requirements, do not necessarily reproduce offspring of the same high quality. However, by continuous and careful selection of the parent cultivars and hand crossing, it is possible to discover which cultivars will produce new cultivars of the standard required. No doubt many pretty seedlings will occur during the process but these should not lead you to believe the standards should be changed to suit them. That can only, in time, lead to the elimination of the type itself. Rather, an extra effort should be made to achieve the reproduction of flowers to the standards required for the various types, to preserve them.

4. **Attractive Colour/s** Self colours, bicolours, blends and variegated flowers may be obtained from crosses of certain other coloured dahlias. The possibilities here are numerous and continued experimentation may lead to desirable results. It may be necessary to adopt line breeding in order to introduce new colours into your seedlings because the parents which produce the form required may produce seedlings all of an almost identical colour, e.g. whites and creams.

5. **Satisfactory Substance of Flowers** Some cultivars have flowers with florets that are leathery to touch and stiff and harsh in appearance. Other cultivars have flowers with florets which are too soft and delicate to be worth growing. These latter are very difficult to handle and have a very short term of life. Somewhere, between these two extremes of substance, lie the more satisfactory flowers which are so attractive and delightful.

6. **Fine Texture of Flowers** Florets with finely grained surfaces are extremely desirable as they add to the bloom a lustre which, in the absence of major faults, must attract favourable attention.

While many of the cultivars of dahlia in existence today have been obtained from natural crossings by bees or other insects, there is much merit in hand pollination. Recording of the cultivars used as parents and the results they produce is essential.

Because all dahlia cultivars are hybrids, rather than pure species, and their past history is unknown, there is a very wide range of characteristics retained within the genes of the plants. Any of these characteristics both desirable and otherwise may recur at any time in seedlings. This helps explain the low percentage of acceptable seedlings.

Certain crossings are more likely to allow desirable characteristics to predominate in the seedlings produced. This applies equally to the plants, tubers and flowers. A completely detailed record of the crossings made and the results obtained can be invaluable in determining the parents to be used in future crosses. There is some likelihood that similar results will be obtained from the parent cultivars which have performed satisfactorily in the past. Thus some measure of prediction, although not very great, can be made based upon the records maintained. This can effectively reduce the number of seedlings required to obtain a comparable number of satisfactory new cultivars.

You can raise a family of seedlings from the same two parent cultivars, over a number of years, with characteristic likenesses. These families of seedlings still have minor distinguishing differences between each of the new cultivars raised.

14 Producing and Gathering Seed

The dahlia belongs to the Compositae plant family which includes many ornamental plants such as the aster, cosmos, calendula, chrysanthemum, helichrysum, gasamia, and zinnia.

It has been understood that dahlia flowers are not self pollinating but there is now reason to doubt this. It was discovered by Paul Sorensen of the United States of America that *Dahlia scapigera* has a reproductive self-compatibility factor. This means that some of our present cultivars could, in fact, be self pollinating and that some crosses which have been fruitful in the past may have been self-pollinated anyway.

However, when hand pollinating, and due to a lack of knowledge of self-compatible cultivars, two genetically distinct cultivars are required to cross-fertilise dahlia seed. This out-breeding means that seedlings of dahlias are not identical to the parent plants.

The pollen is collected from the ripe pistil with a fine painting brush with soft hair. The pistils ripen from the outside of the disc centre in rotation over a few days until the centre is reached. Late in the mornings when the weather is warm, the sacks holding the pollen burst open and a fine powdery substance which is yellow or orange coloured appears. This is collected with the brush and will adhere to it. It is best transferred fresh to the stigma of the mother flower immediately, but it can be placed in a glass or plastic tube, sealed, labelled and kept in a refrigerator at 5°C for a week or two and used as required. Alternatively, the male flower can be picked and kept in a room as a cut flower and the pollen collected and used as it ripens. The stigma is a fine thread-like growth appearing at the base of the inner florets and amongst the pistils in the disc centre of the bloom. The end of the stigma is an open ''Y'' shaped growth. The pollen on the brush is very gently brushed over the open stigma. The stigma is sticky when receptive and the pollen will adhere to it. If the two cultivars are compatible the cross will take. It is, however, advisable to repeat the cross for about three consecutive days to ensure that it is made satisfactorily.

If you should have a very good new seedling amongst this year's batch, there is no reason why it cannot be used as either one of the parent cultivars in your crossings.

To ensure that the hand crossing you made is the one which actually fertilises the seed, it is necessary to cover both of the flowers to be used as parents prior to their maturity. A light-weight, fine mesh material like a nylon stocking is suitable for this purpose. Plastic covering which excludes air circulation could cause condensation of moisture inside it and rot the seed pod. The covering is required to prevent bees and other insects from carrying unwanted pollen from other flowers and depositing it on the parent flowers. The female parent flower must remain covered after the crossing has been made in case it does not take. Then a bee is able to make another crossing with pollen collected elsewhere, and this would spoil your records.

Many growers are hand pollinating dahlias today in the hope that they will breed better cultivars. However, other growers are raising cultivars better than those already in existence by collecting naturally crossed seed. The improvement of the various types of dahlia should be the objective of every seedling grower. Seedlings kept should be as near as possible to the standards in order to preserve the types.

Some dahlia flowers fail to produce seed while others are very prolific seed bearers. The number of florets in a flower has a direct relationship to its seed productivity. A flower with a tightly closed centre and many florets, does not usually produce seeds. Open centre types with their disc-shaped centres with many of their reproductive parts exposed produce a large number of seeds. It follows that if you are growing the open centre types, Orchid and Collarette, it is most likely that they will dominate any natural crossings made by bees or insects in your garden.

Temperature and day length control the number of florets in dahlia flowers. Early in the flowering season, when the number of daylight hours is greater and the temperature is warmer, during late summer and early autumn, the blooms formed have more florets in them and double types seldom open their centres. However, as the season progresses to late autumn, the number of daylight hours is less and the temperature is lower. The plants respond to this warning of their approaching dormancy by producing flowers with less florets and open centres in which are exposed their reproductive parts in their endeavour to survive.

Unfortunately, the moist atmosphere of autumn also brings to many areas fungal diseases which thrive upon the dying florets and ripening seed pods and quickly destroy them. To combat this problem, it is wise to carefully pluck the florets from the blooms, retaining only the pods of seed on the plant. The pods need to remain on the plants until the seed is fully developed but not necessarily thoroughly ripened. They can be picked when they start to turn a straw green colour and the seed can be felt by gently pressing the pods between the thumb and the fingers. In the meantime, covers should be used, if necessary, to keep the pods dry, but the air must be allowed to circulate around them.

If your environment is free from fungal diseases and has suitable climatic conditions which allow the seed pods to fully ripen on the bushes, then allow them to do so. When the pods are fully developed and mature, the bracts will spring open and scatter the seed on the garden bed. So it is necessary to continually inspect the pods and harvest the seeds as soon as they are in the most satisfactory condition.

After picking, the pods should be opened, the seed separated from the bracts and other debris, then allowed to dry on a sheet of paper for a day or two before being placed in a packet, box or jar for winter storage.

15 Growing Seedlings

Early in spring, when the danger of frost has passed, the seed can be sown. It can be planted in the garden bed or in seed boxes. Very early plantings can be made under glass or plastic. If necessary, bottom heat can be supplied to the seed bed to encourage quicker germination in cooler weather.

A soil which drains very freely could be used in the seed boxes. However, to reduce the possibility of losses of plants due to damping off under the warm humid conditions, it would be wise to use a specially prepared mixture of two-thirds perlite or vermiculite and one-third peatmoss.

The seed should be covered to a depth of approximately 12 mm and kept moist. As soon as the young plants can be handled, they should be pricked out of the seed box and planted into a suitable general potting mixture with a pH reading around 6.5 in small pots. To avoid this step of potting, the seed needs to be sown with at least 50 mm spacing both ways. The plants should be hardened off in a cool protected area for at least a week before planting out into the garden bed.

Seedlings are usually planted about 230 mm apart in rows which are a similar width apart. They are planted close to either give a mass effect when

A bed of seedlings

flowering or to allow for the majority of the plants being removed when they produce poor quality flowers. All plants you wish to keep for another season should be staked and labelled with regard to their size, type and colour immediately they start to flower so that they are not passed over or pulled out later.

Seedlings flower during their first season's growth just as green plants and tubers do. They also produce a clump of tubers for the next season. Propagation from then onwards is exactly the same as that of named cultivars.

When the buds of seedlings begin to open, every one of them is a potential champion of its type. They provide a wonderful source of enjoyment to their growers. Naturally, some conform to the standard requirements for exhibition purposes while others are attractive but not of any particular standard type and others again are not satisfactory at all.

It is easy to discard unsatisfactory seedlings but those which fall just short of the requirements tend to be kept in case they improve. Consequently, tubers of many of the ''pretty'' flowers are passed on or sold to other growers. They can be a source of disappointment to unsuspecting exhibitors who are not very discriminating in their choice of new cultivars to add to their collection.

The percentage of good quality seedlings, those worth growing again, is very low, especially if they are from natural crossings made by bees rather than hand pollination. It therefore requires a good deal of patience to continue growing them each year. However, the appearance of one or two very good ones, occasionally, will spur you on for years to come. Of course, there are those gardeners who plant seedlings of dahlias just for their mass colour effect in the garden then discard them after their flowering season. The dwarf bedding dahlia seedlings which are available in several different mixtures are ideal for this purpose and their short plants do not require staking.

16 Pests and Diseases

Pests

If any insects, mites, worms, grubs, snails or slugs are present in your garden, they are likely to attack your dahlia plants. It should be your aim to prevent these pests from increasing by maintaining a clean garden. Undesirable and unhealthy vegetative material should not be buried in the soil nor placed in a compost heap. As it is unsuitable for composting, it should be burned or removed and destroyed. The soil should be cultivated to eliminate weeds. Overhead watering is very helpful in the control of insects, particularly the dreaded red spider. Frequent examination and manual removal of worms and grubs from your plants should be practised. Whenever you are working amongst or admiring your plants keep an eye on them for these pests and kill any you find. Avoid bringing in insect infested straw and manures from other areas. Pay particular attention to ailing or spent crops of tomatoes, beans, cucumbers, egg plants, members of the marrow and pumpkin family, cabbages, sprouts, cauliflowers, zinnias or chrysanthemums because they will harbour insects. In fact, all spent or ailing crops should be removed promptly and disposed of to keep your garden clean.

Certain herb plants should be grown as deterrents and herbal sprays used. Predatory insects, such as ladybirds and praying mantis, and birds should be encouraged.

Attend to your plants so that they are growing vigorously and healthily. Any diseased plants should be removed and burnt immediately upon detection. Leaving them in your dahlia bed will spread the disease rapidly. This applies to fungal diseases and the various virus diseases which infect dahlias.

Unfortunately, although there are many chemical sprays available to control different insects, most of them become ineffective if used continuously. The insects build up immunity to the chemical. Then a new chemical spray has to be used to maintain a check upon the insect. Many of these chemicals are very dangerous to use and protective clothing and masks are essential when using them. Residual chemicals in the soil can render it unusable for vegetable growing.

In fifty years I have seldom used these dangerous chemicals and then only early in my dahlia growing. One very dry season my experience with DDT convinced me that there must be other ways of dealing with insect pests. I had a heavy infestation of an insect, probably aphids. I sprayed with DDT, the "cure all" of the day. Shortly afterwards, nearly all my plants were covered with red spider so badly that many of them actually died.

Borderspray jets which water over the foliage but below the flowers contribute considerably to control of insects. Dry weather and dry plants are very susceptible to insect infestation.

Diseases

There are two main categories of diseases in dahlias: fungal and viral. They can be carried in the tubers of the plants to the following season. Infected plants will also spread these diseases if allowed to remain in your dahlia patch. Fungal diseases are often airborne and their presence is undesirable. They can infest the soil and affect future plantings there.

Powdery Mildew can spoil plants if it is present early in their life or flowering season. To prevent this occurring early in the growing season, place plants further apart to allow more air to circulate between them. Thick foliage coverage between the plants will contribute to the mildew's early appearance. Often, if weather conditions are suitable, it will appear late in the season and spread rapidly throughout the bed. It is airborne and the spores settle on damp foliage and spread. Lime sulphur dusting powder or a sulphur spray will assist control.

It is recommended that all waste dahlia plant material be burnt or destroyed whether or not it is considered to be healthy. It should not be turned into the soil nor placed on the compost heap in case a soil borne disease is present.

Symptoms of viral diseases are difficult to separate from some of the symptoms of plant food deficiencies. Microscopic examination of the plant tissue will determine the presence of viral diseases. If in doubt, any plants which do not respond in due time to dressings of corrective fertilisers should be removed and burnt. Cutting tools and aphids carry the disease from plant to plant by transferring the sap. After use, tools should be sterilised or disinfected before using them on another plant. Take care when pruning with your fingers not to carry any sap to the next plant. There is no cure for these diseases, so infected plants are not only useless but their retention will quickly spread the disease to others.

Viral Disease	Symptoms
Vein Mosaic Vein Mottling or Vein Clearing	Light green or yellow spots along veins. Blotchy, localised or quite general, appearing chlorotic but along the veins as well. Stipple chlorosis can be mistaken for Vein Clearing virus but it is between the veins as well as along them.
Rosetting or Rosette Rugosity	Leaves smaller than usual, wrinkled generally, very close together creating a rosette. Grey green foliage. It can appear on one or two laterals at first but it usually stunts the whole plant.
Local Lesion Neurosis	Small necrotic areas, sometimes like spray burn spots on apples.

Viral Disease	Symptoms
Leaf Distortion	Sometimes connected with Local Lesion Neurosis. Unequal development of two halves of leaf. Leaf skews to the side.
Leaf Curl	Complete downward turn of leaf.
Leaf Roll	Margins of leaves revolute (turned downwards).
Rugose Mosaic	Puckering of leaves, wrinkled, creating a series of raised patches.
Stunting	Lack of vigour, stunting effect.
Foliation	Few or even no flower buds set flowers.
Colour Breaks	Streaking of flowers, slightly bleached. Chance variegation.
Asymmetrical Blooms	Drooping florets, disfigured centres.
Root-Shoot Proliferation	Clusters of up to 10 or 12 shoots instead of the customary one or two.
Root Deformation	Thickened and shorter roots.
Cracks in Roots	Brownish cracks in neck and root of tubers. Poor keeping quality of infected tubers.

17 Exhibiting

Selecting and Cutting Blooms

Exhibitors of dahlias are enthusiastic about the growing of their flowers and spend much of their leisure time among their plants. In the week before a show, each bud is carefully watched as it opens in the hope that it will provide a first-class bloom for the show bench. This assists the grower in nominating the classes in which he wishes to show and ensures that he knows just where his best flowers are when the time comes to pick them.

. When picking the various kinds of dahlias, it is advisable to have a set of size rings with you. This will enable you to discard oversized blooms. Flowers with brush centres, that is, all the centre florets growing out together to form a brush-like rather than cone-shaped centre, twisted stems, and blooms which are badly bleached or burnt, should all be discarded. As the flowers are picked, it is a good idea to have ready a container holding cold water in which the blooms can be placed. They should be picked in the cool of the evening the night before the show and conditioned to be ready for handling the next day.

Stems should be cut 40 to 45 cm long wherever possible even if it is necessary to sacrifice a few buds. Larger-flowered cultivars will have been pruned for at least that length and there are usually plenty of buds to follow on on the smaller-flowered ones.

A can with a hole cut in the side to allow stems to pass through is ideal for scalding. It should be the size of a preserved fruit can or larger. It can be placed on the stove and kept simmering while one or two stems are scalded at a time. The steam and heat from the boiling water will pass upwards while the blooms are held at an angle and as far as possible from the heat. Place 20 mm of the cut end of the stem in the boiling water for half to one minute.

After scalding, place the blooms in deep containers of cold water and store them in the coolest place available where they will not be in a draught.

Now the blooms can be examined more closely. Blade, twisted, damaged, and burnt florets can be removed and the best blooms sorted into their collections ready for staging. Blooms with gaps in the floret formation can be improved by carefully rearranging the florets, pulling some to one side and some to the other side to fill the gap. Shallow blooms can be increased in depth by gently stroking the florets of the flower backwards while the bloom is held securely at the back with the other hand. Very careful handling of the blooms while working on them is necessary because bruising or other damage could render them useless.

Rise early on show morning to give yourself plenty of time for final preparations, and to make sure you arrive at the show with enough time to stage your blooms. Many exhibitors spend all night with their blooms and some who travel long distances to the shows transport their blooms at night to allow them sufficient time to stage them well. Time permitting, as soon as it is light enough, have a quick look over your plants for the odd flower which you may have missed. If you find one, pick it, scald the stem, and place it among those you have sorted the night before. The flowers will all be open now and can quickly be rechecked as they are packed for transporting to the show. Always take a few spares with you in case one or two throw open their centres or are damaged in transit.

Packing and Transporting Blooms

For many years, I have used gallon paint tins in which are placed two layers of fine-mesh wire about 75 mm apart, to carry my flowers to shows. I have found that this way they will carry over long distances with little if any damage. The tins are filled with water to within about 25 mm of the top. This provides sufficient weight to prevent them from moving in the car, with careful driving. The lip on the paint tin stops the water from splashing out.

Another good means of conveyance is to place the flowers in bottles, plug them, then stand them in crates.

Some exhibitors use plastic containers with water in them and strap the stems of the blooms to the side of the container. A support of wire or bamboo is placed against the stems to keep them straight and firm.

A wooden framework in the vehicle to prevent the containers from moving would be an added advantage, especially in the event of unexpected sudden braking.

Staging of Blooms

Colours

In staging a collection of flowers in tiers, remember that the dark colours stand out if they are used at the back.

The blooms should be so placed as to complement each other. Self-colours should be placed in groupings such as purple, mauve, cream; scarlet, pink and white. Self-colours can be used to accentuate less prominent similar tonings in blends and bi-coloured flowers; for example, a flower with white at the base of the florets and the remainder flushed mauve-pink will be complemented by placing a white self-coloured flower next to it.

Where possible avoid one flower dominating another, a bloom with a glowing colour should not be placed next to one without lustre as it will make the latter look drab and unattractive. Particular attention should be given to your best blooms so that they do not escape the judge's eye. You will also need to take into account the exhibits on either side of yours, so that your good bloom is not overshadowed by a bright colour shown by an opponent.

The Angle of the Flower

The angle at which the flower has grown to the stem also has a bearing on where it will be placed in an exhibit. For instance, a flower grown parallel to the stem is most suitable at the back, at 45 degrees to the stem in the centre, and at 90 degrees to the stem (flat on top) in the front. In this way all flowers are placed where they can be seen with comparative ease. See the reference to "neck stretchers" on page 43 as this applies particularly to the larger-flowered types. A 45 degree angle is considered the ideal position of the bloom on the stem except Pompon type which is straight upward.

Plugging

Among the suitable plugging materials to hold the stem secure in the container are dahlia stalks, corks, rhubarb stems and wooden wedges with grooves to take the stems. Avoid materials which are too soft to hold the bloom firmly. The lower portion of the plug should be wedge-shaped so that as it is pressed into the top of the container against the stem, it grips and holds it rigid. Then when the judge picks up the container to examine the bloom closely, it will remain in position. Plugs may require re-cutting, or two or more plugs may be used in large-necked containers. Do not press too hard when plugging, as stem damage can result and it may be difficult to place the bloom in a satisfactory position afterwards. The container should be topped up with water to ensure a sufficient supply, especially for two-day shows.

Requirements for Flower Pot Dahlias

Flower pot dahlias are intended to display the grower's ability to produce a well balanced plant, staked with either one Giant or Large size flower on the plant; or, a well balanced bush of evenly spaced laterals each staked individually to maintain their position and each carrying a flower at its terminal for Medium and Small size flowers. Miniatures and other small flowered cultivars are shown as a bush in full flower. The greater the mass of flowers in bloom at the time of exhibition, the better. These plants are stopped and a greater number of laterals allowed to develop. Very little disbudding is done and only the side buds are removed as the flowers begin to open to ensure that the flowers are not oversize. Good, clean, healthy foliage is essential.

Transporting these flower pot dahlias can be a problem due to their height, and they cannot be carried lying on their side because the stems could bend to an upright position in a short time.

Flower pot dahlias make a very pleasing exhibit and, of course, are more likely to stay in fresh condition.

Points to Remember

• Spray your flowers with cool, clean water to keep them fresh and encourage them to reach their peak when being judged.

• Name your flowers legibly to assist others in choosing cultivars to grow in future and those reporting on the show.

• After judging, listen carefully to the judge's comments on all the exhibits. This will help you in selecting cultivars to grow or discard, and in correcting any irregularities in staging, all of which will bring added success at future shows.

18 Appreciation of Dahlia Blooms

It is most important that dahlia growers receive enjoyment and satisfaction from their flowers. The Standard Requirements of Perfection set by the Australian Dahlia Council appear on pages 62 to 65. They list the upper and lower limits of the diameter size for each group of flowers and describe the floret formation of the various types of dahlia, colour, condition, stem and staging requirements. These standards are used to evaluate the quality of dahlia blooms in Australia. It is neither possible nor desirable to describe exactly all the requirements of perfect flowers because there are minor variations in the form and build of the flowers between cultivars. Beauty is also in the eyes of the beholder. This gives rise to different interpretations of the standard requirements. However, in spite of these factors, reasonable consistency does exist in the evaluation of blooms staged on show benches in Australia.

To gain a better appreciation of the dahlias which you grow, it is recommended that you study the Standard Requirements, and also the sketches of floret forms on pages 60–1.

In addition to the dahlias covered by these standards, there are many cultivars used for garden display purposes. Colour and an abundance of blooms are required. Although these blooms may not conform with the A.D.C. Standard Requirements of any particular type, they are very attractive in the garden. To recognise these cultivars and add more interest for the public, some show schedules cater for these flowers in a separate section of the show. Certain adjustments to the Standard Requirements are necessary to evaluate these blooms. Therefore, in place of conformity with the requirements of form of the types, the following characteristics are considered to be more appropriate.

Drawing Attention

Blooms should be unusual, fancy, rare or out of the ordinary in their form, colour and/or condition.

Holding Attention

Blooms should be exceptional, distinguished, matchless and/or choice in their form, colour and/or condition.

Arrangement

Blooms should be arranged to their best advantage and to display their beauty. The mass effect of a number of blooms of the same cultivar in a container should add to their attractiveness. Clean healthy foliage attached to the stems should be preferred to bare stems of flowers.

Standard form specimen blooms are those with floret formations as near as possible to the Standard Requirements of Perfection. The addition of a section for garden display blooms at a show allows growers of these flowers to enter into competition without confusing the public regarding types of dahlias in the specimen bloom section. They are staged in multiple numbers in a vase. This allows more attention to be devoted to the form of the single specimen blooms. Show committees can do much to pass on knowledge of the various types of dahlia by arranging their show schedule classes in an orderly manner, which should be followed through to the show benches. Refer to basic show schedule on pages 69 to 70.

When specimens of blooms are staged in multiple numbers in one container, attention needs to be given to the matching of size, condition and colour. Consequently, usually less attention is paid to the form of the flowers. As it is practically impossible to obtain three or more flowers of a cultivar that match in every respect, the competition between growers becomes one of the exhibitors' showmanship, rather than a competition between the flowers themselves. The flowers should reveal the careful cultivation and attention to detail provided by their growers.

Floret Forms as Described by the Australian Dahlia Council

Ball and Pompon Types

All florets should be involute (edges turned upwards). The tips of the florets should appear to be rounded. The back florets of the bloom should reflex (turn back sharply under themselves) to the stem.

tips rounded

reflexed floret

Orchid Type

Centre should be open with fresh pollen and disc-shaped. Surrounding the centre there should be eight straight and involute (edges turned upwards) florets which show a distinct (noticeably different) colour on the involute reverse side.

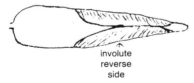

involute reverse side

Stellar Type

Centre should be closed and dome-shaped breaking gradually with involute (edges turned upwards) immature florets to (two or three rows of) fully developed outer florets. Outer florets should be straight, narrow and involute and show a distinct (noticeably different) colour on the involute reverse side.

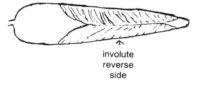

involute reverse side

Nymphea Type

Centre should be closed and dome-shaped breaking gradually to preferably five rows of fully developed outer florets. Outer florets should be broad and slightly cupped (whole edge of floret raised slightly) with rounded ends. The layers of florets should be openly spaced to give a delicate and light appearance.

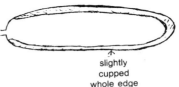

slightly cupped whole edge

Formal Decorative Type

The florets near the centre may be involute (edges turned upwards) but those further away should be broad, smooth and flat. The tips of the florets may be either rounded or pointed. The back florets should recurve (gradually curve backwards) towards the stem.

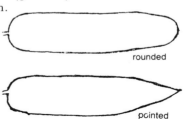

rounded

pointed

Informal Decorative Type

Outer florets should be broad, flat and slightly twisty, wavy or revolute (edges turned downwards) for less than one-quarter of the length of any floret. The tips of the florets should preferably be pointed. The back florets should preferably recurve towards the stem.

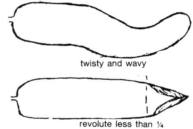

twisty and wavy

revolute less than ¼

Semi-cactus Type

Centre should be closed, high and cone-shaped breaking gradually with flat, pointed immature florets to outer florets. Outer florets should be broad and flat towards the base half and revolute (edges turned downwards) from the pointed tips for more than one-quarter but for less than half of their length. The florets may be either slightly incurved (gradually curved forwards towards the face of the bloom) or straight.

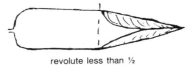

revolute less than ½

Fimbriated Type

Bloom should have all its florets from the centre to the back fimbriated (deeply split) from the tips at least 10 mm and in proportion to its size. In all other requirements the bloom should be a replica (reproduction) of one of the approved types. *Note:* Serrated (shallowly split) tips of florets are a fault in a bloom.

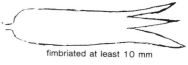

fimbriated at least 10 mm

Cactus Type

Centre should be closed, high and cone-shaped breaking gradually with narrow and partly revolute (edges turned downwards) immature florets to outer florets. Outer florets should be narrow, preferably with revolute edges overlapping from the tips for at least two thirds of their length and preferably pointed. The florets may be either slightly incurved (gradually curved forwards towards the face of the bloom) or straight.

revolute at least ⅔

Collarette Type

Centre should be open with fresh pollen and disc-shaped. Surrounding the centre there should be a collar of wavy florets with multiple divisions, usually pointed at the tip of each division and preferably half the length of the outer florets, which should be eight in number, broad, flat and rounded at the ends, and overlap to form two rows. The colours of the collar florets and the outer florets should preferably contrast (noticeably different).

collar

Pincer/Exhibition Cactus Type

Centre should be closed, high and cone-shaped breaking gradually with very narrow and revolute (edges turned downwards) immature florets to outer florets. Outer florets should be very narrow, long and pointed with revolute edges overlapping for as near as possible to their whole length. Towards the tips, the florets should be strongly incurved (turned back sharply over themselves towards the centre of the bloom) and may also regularly turn to one side.

strongly incurved

Anemone Type

Centre should have a dense group of tubular florets surrounded by preferably one row of regularly arranged, flat, broad florets with rounded ends.

dense group of tubular florets

Exhibition Standards for Specimen Blooms

The specialist dahlia societies in each State of Australia have joined together to form the Australian Dahlia Council. Conferences are held annually by the A.D.C. in different States on a rotational basis. This allows growers to meet their interstate counterparts and generally discuss dahlia matters in both a formal and informal manner. Because the distances between States precludes many members from attending meetings, the business of the A.D.C. is conducted by correspondence, which gives most members an opportunity to participate.

The A.D.C. published an *Australian Guide to Dahlias* in 1980. The Guide contains the standards and some information to assist people in their interpretation of them. Unlike other countries, Australia does not rely upon a list of cultivars which classifies dahlias by size and type. These lists are unsatisfactory in Australia because:

1. They presume that cultivars will not change in their size or form, both of which we have found they do here. We do have to contend with a wide range of climates and soils. We don't want to exclude too many good flowers from our show benches nor lower our standards to permit substandard flowers to be shown.

2. The use of "tolerance" of oversize blooms in the size ranges makes a farce of the preclassification system and encourages additional forcing of plants. It also lessens the chances of winning with blooms of the size range.

3. Many unworthy cultivars are classified to the nearest type merely to make it possible to exhibit them. Once they are classified, very little attention is given to their form by judges. Consequently, the blooms on the show bench do not clearly depict the type of dahlia that they are supposed to represent. This encourages the breeding of cut flowers rather than true to type dahlias.

4. Classification lists remove the incentive for people to study and understand the type requirements because that is done for them. Blooms that are not true to form give a distorted image of the type.

The standards to which we adhere in Australia are as follows:

Australian Dahlia Council's Standard Requirements of Perfection of Dahlia Blooms for assessing the Relative Quality of Dahlia Blooms Exhibited at Floricultural Shows held in Australia.

Formation of Blooms Requirements

Pompon Type
Bloom should be fully double, symmetrical and spherical like a golf ball. Centre should be closed, fully developed and as high as the surrounding face florets. Florets should preferably be uniform in size throughout the bloom. All florets should be involute, regularly arranged and neat in appearance. The tips of the florets should appear to be rounded. The back florets of the bloom should reflex to the stem. Colour plates 11–15.

Ball Type
Bloom should be fully double, symmetrical and spherical like a ball. Centre should be closed, fully developed and as high as the surrounding face florets. Florets should preferably be uniform in size throughout the bloom. All florets should be involute, regularly arranged and neat in appearance. The tips of the florets should appear to be rounded. The back florets of the bloom should reflex to the stem. Plates 1–10.

Formal Decorative Type
Bloom should be fully double, symmetrical and at least half but not more than its diameter in depth. Face view should be circular in outline, regular in arrangement and neat in appearance. Centre should be closed, fully developed and as high as the surrounding face florets, breaking gradually with immature florets. Near the centre they may be involute but those further away should be broad, smooth and flat. The tips of the florets may be either rounded or pointed. The back florets should recurve towards the stem. Plates 31–50.

Informal Decorative Type

Bloom should be fully double, symmetrical and at least half but not more than its diameter in depth. Face view should be circular in outline, regular in arrangement and neat in appearance. Centre should be closed, high and cone-shaped breaking gradually with immature florets which near the centre should be broad and almost flat. Outer florets should be broad, flat, and slightly twisty, wavy or revolute for less than one-quarter of the length of any floret. The tips of the florets should preferably be pointed. The back florets should preferably recurve towards the stem. Plates 51–70.

Semi-cactus Type

Bloom should be fully double, symmetrical and at least half but not more than its diameter in depth. Face view should be circular in outline, regular in arrangement and neat in appearance. Centre should be closed, high and cone-shaped breaking gradually with flat, pointed immature florets to outer florets. Outer florets should be broad and flat towards the base half and revolute from the pointed tips for more than one-quarter but for less than half of their length. The florets may be either slightly incurved or straight. Plates 71–95.

Cactus Type

Bloom should be fully double, symmetrical and at least half but not more than its diameter in depth. Face view should be circular in outline, regular in arrangement and neat in appearance. Centre should be closed, high and cone-shaped, breaking gradually with narrow and partly revolute immature florets to outer florets. Outer florets should be narrow, preferably with revolute edges overlapping from the tips for at least two-thirds of their length and preferably pointed. The florets may be either slightly incurved or straight. Plates 96–120.

Pincer Type or Exhibition Cactus Type

Bloom should be fully double, symmetrical and approximately half its diameter in depth. Face view should be circular in outline, regular in arrange-ment and neat in appearance. Centre should be closed, high and cone-shaped, breaking gradually with very narrow and revolute immature florets to outer florets. Outer florets should be very narrow, long and pointed with revolute edges overlapping for as near as possible to their whole length. Towards the tips, the florets should be strongly incurved and may also regularly turn to one side. Plates 121–5 and 134–5.

Fimbriated Type

Bloom should have all its florets from the centre to the back fimbriated from the tips at least 10 mm and in proportion to its size. In all other requirements the bloom should be a replica of one of the approved types. Plates 126–133.

Nymphea Type

Bloom should be fully double, and symmetrical. Side view should be saucer-shaped and face view should be circular in outline, and regular in arrangement. The layers of florets should be openly spaced to give a delicate and light appearance. Centre should be closed and dome-shaped breaking gradually to preferably five rows of fully developed outer florets. Outer florets should be broad and slightly cupped with rounded ends. Plates 26–30.

Anemone Type

Bloom should be fully double and symmetrical. Side view should be dome-shaped in outline and face view should be circular in outline. Centre should have a dense group of tubular florets surrounded by preferably one row of regularly arranged, flat, broad florets with rounded ends. Plates 136–9.

Orchid Type

Bloom should be symmetrical with side view flat. Face view should be circular in outline, regular in arrangement and neat in appearance. Centre should be open with fresh pollen and disc-shaped. Surrounding the centre there should be eight straight and involute florets which show a distinct colour on the involute reverse side. Plates 16–20.

Stellar Type

Bloom should be fully double, symmetrical with side view flat. Face view should be circular in outline, regularly arranged and neat in appearance. Centre should be closed and dome-shaped breaking gradually with involute immature florets to fully developed outer florets. Outer florets should be straight, narrow and involute and show a distinct colour on the involute reverse side. Plates 21–5.

Collarette Type

Bloom should be symmetrical with side view almost flat. Face view should be circular in outline, regular in arrangement and neat in appearance. Centre should be open with fresh pollen and disc-shaped. Surrounding the centre there should be a collar of wavy florets with multiple divisions usually pointed at the tip of each division and preferably half the length of the outer florets which should be eight in number, broad, flat, rounded at the ends and overlap to form two rows. The colours of the collar florets and the outer florets should preferably contrast. Plates 140–3.

Other Requirements

Stem
The stem should be straight, situated centrally to the bloom, rigid and round with length to the first node and thickness in proportion to the size of the bloom it carries. Artificial support is prohibited. It should be cut at least 300 mm long, except Pompon which may be 230 mm long. It should be staged with at least 160 mm protruding from the container. The stem should carry the bloom (facing upward) at a 45 degree angle, except Pompon which should face straight upward in line with the stem.

Condition
Bloom should be perfectly fresh and mature. It should be of firm substance and fine in texture. It should also be clean and free from blemish.

Colour
The colour of a bloom should be clear, bright and attractive. The colours of a bloom of a bi-coloured, blend or variegated cultivar should be evenly marked.

List of Colour Groups

Based upon the Royal Horticultural Society of England's colour chart.

Yellow to Orange	Yellow, yellow orange, orange, orange white, greyed yellow (light brown tones), greyed orange (dark brown tones), grey brown and brown.
Pink to Red	Greyed orange (pink tones), orange red, greyed red (dark pink tones) and red.
Dark Red to Purple	Red purple (dark red tones), purple, greyed purple (dark purple red tones).
Lavender to Violet	Violet blue (lavender tones), purple violet, violet.

White	White, yellow white (cream tones).
Bi-colours	Two clearly defined and sharply changing colours on the face of the florets forming a regular pattern.
Blends of colours	Two or more colours which merge gradually or intermingle but are distinguishable from a distance of two metres.
Variegated colours	A ground colour striped, spotted or splashed with a distinctly different colour.

Colour Abbreviations

YO	Yellow to orange
PR	Pink to red
DkRP	Dark red to purple
LV	Lavender to violet
W	White
Bi	Bi-colour
BL	Blend
Var	Variegated

Size Requirements

Size groups

Diameter limits	Names	Types of dahlias to which applicable
Over 90 mm	Large	Ball
50 mm to 90 mm	Small	
Under 50 mm	—	Pompon
Over 260 mm	Giant	Formal Decorative
210 mm to 260 mm	Large	Informal Decorative
160 mm to 210 mm	Medium	Semi-cactus
120 mm to 160 mm	Small	Cactus
Under 120 mm	Miniature	
Over 160 mm	Large	Pincer/Exhibition
Under 160 mm	Small	Cactus
		Fimbriated
Under 160 mm	—	Nymphea
		Collarette
Under 120 mm	—	Anemone
		Orchid
		Stellar

Staging Requirements

Exhibits should be attractive and appealing in appearance and of matching height. Blooms should be firmly plugged in containers at a uniform and acceptable height, placed facing viewers and named. Foliage should be healthy, fresh, clean and free from blemish.

List of Sizes and Types of Dahlias

Sizes	Types
Large	Ball
Small	Ball
	Pompon
Giant	Formal Decorative
Large	Formal Decorative
Medium	Formal Decorative
Small	Formal Decorative
Miniature	Formal Decorative
Giant	Informal Decorative
Large	Informal Decorative
Medium	Informal Decorative
Small	Informal Decorative
Miniature	Informal Decorative
Giant	Semi-cactus
Large	Semi-cactus
Medium	Semi-cactus
Small	Semi-cactus
Miniature	Semi-cactus
Giant	Cactus
Large	Cactus
Medium	Cactus
Small	Cactus
Miniature	Cactus
Large	Pincer or Exhibition Cactus
Small	Pincer or Exhibition Cactus
Large	Fimbriated
Small	Fimbriated
	Nymphea
	Collarette
	Anemone
	Orchid
	Stellar

There are 13 types of dahlia. Some have two sizes, others have five sizes. The total number of sizes and types is 32.

Glossary of Terms

Attractive bedding dahlias Appealing, pleasant Dwarf border singles, Dwarf Redskin semi doubles with reddish foliage and Hi-Dolly semi doubles.

Blend Two or more colours which merge gradually or intermingle but are distinguishable from a distance of two metres.

Bloom The flowerhead including florets, bracts, and calyx. The sparkle, sheen and brilliance on the surface of the plant and flowerhead.

Bract A small scale-like leaf which accompanies each flower.

Breaking gradually Opening with undeveloped florets of varying or increasing size until fully developed florets are reached.

Brush centre A mass of florets of the same length making up the centre. The tips of these centre florets look like a brush.

Cacti Plants belonging to the Order Cactaceae which are not related to dahlias.

Calyx The outer set of perianth segments which are green.

Circular Round, like a ring.

Class The order in which exhibits are to be staged. The requirements for one group of comparable exhibits (dahlias).

Classification Allot to a group of the same size and type of dahlia for reference purposes.

Closed centre A group of undeveloped florets completely cover the centre of the bloom closing it from view.

Coarseness Rough, gross, unbalanced in proportion.

Collection More than one size and/or type of dahlia grouped in a class or garden.

Cone-shaped Round at the base and coming to a point at the top. Note: florets with pointed tips unopened form a cone-shaped centre.

Confusion Confusing appearance of irregular patterns caused by florets growing in varied directions; irregular, inconsistent formation.

Contrast Noticeably different from.

Cultivar A cultivated variety.

Cupped Hollowed—see Involute.

Disc centre Flat, round shaped centre.

Disc florets The small tubular floral parts which make up the central part of the flower-head.

Display An exhibit in which attractiveness of arrangement and general effort is of prime importance.

Dome-shaped Semi circular, half circular. Note: florets with rounded ends usually have closed dome-shaped centres.

Dwarf Dahlias which normally grow less than 60 cm in height.

Entry An exhibit in a class at a show.

Even Equal, level, smooth, uniform in quality, proportionately or equally balanced.

Fine Excellent, good, opposite to coarse; disproportionately narrow florets.

Fimbriated A natural border of tattered ends of florets adorning the bloom. Deep lacerations. Note: shallowly split tips of florets known as serrations are a fault in a bloom.

Floret The conspicuously coloured leaves which build a dahlia bloom and allow its size and type to be determined.

Flower The reproductive organs of higher plants.

Fluted Grooved—see Involute.

Foliage The leaves and the stems supporting them.

Form The shape of the blooms. Certain characteristics of the form of dahlia blooms determine their type.

Fully double Multiple rows of florets and closed centre of undeveloped florets.

Garden cultivar Cultivars with attractive attributes but lacking sufficient of the ideal standards to successfully compete with cultivars of the same classification.

Gradually incurved A slow but steady curve forward towards the face of the bloom.

High centre A centre as high as the surrounding face florets.

Hybrid A plant derived from the interbreeding of two or more species.

Ideal Perfect. The highest conception of standard for imitation.

Incurved Florets which towards the tip gradually curve forward toward the face of the bloom.

Involute The marginal edges of florets rolled or folded upward.

Kind Group of plants, flowers or vegetables, e.g. chrysanthemums, dahlias, roses, peaches, pears, plums, onions or parsnips.

Lateral   A side shoot of a plant.

Margin   The area adjacent to the edge of a floret.

Neat   Tidy, well shaped, proportionately balanced, opposite to coarse.

Petal   Coloured leaf forming part of a bloom or flower but without a pistil—see Floret.

Pompon   Bunch of threads round in shape attached to a cap. Note: pompone is an incorrect spelling.

Quilled   Tubular, round like a pipe. The centre florets of Anemone type dahlias are tubular—see Revolute.

Recurve   To turn back towards the stem. Outer florets which toward the tip gradually curve backward toward the stem of the bloom.

Reflex   Recurve on itself. Outer florets which toward the tip quickly curve backward toward their base.

Regular   Even, uniform or consistent patterns.

Revolute   The marginal edges of florets rolled or folded downward.

Rigid   Not easily bent.

Saucer-shaped   Round with the whole edge raised slightly.

Shallow   Not deep, of little depth.

Seedling   A plant produced from seed. A dahlia plant raised from seed until it is named. It is recommended that seedlings should be either named or discarded after the third flowering season and can be named earlier for identification purposes.

Semi   Half one and half another type of dahlia eg. Semi-cactus is part Decorative and part Cactus types.

Serrated   Shallowly split tips of florets. A fault in a bloom.

Size   A measurement which allows blooms to be grouped into comparable classes for exhibition.

Slightly incurved   Not much curvature forward toward the centre of a bloom.

Species   A group of closely related plants, e.g. *Dahlia coccinea* or *Dahlia variabilis*.

Spherical   Round from all points of view, like a ball in shape.

Sport   Occasionally a cultivar will produce a bloom of different colouring from normal. It is said to have sported. The grower can try to separate that portion of the plant which has produced the different coloured bloom from the rest of the plant. If this is successful, and the blooms are consistently of a different colour, then it can be treated as a seedling until it is named. Sports can either revert to the original colour or be produced by other plants of the same cultivar in a different garden.

Stalk   Main axis of a plant from the roots to the flower.

Standard   A description of the perfect bloom or state of a bloom generally accepted as being worthy of imitation. The objective toward which dahlias are grown for exhibition purposes.

Stem   Main axis of a plant, a twig supporting a bloom.

Stiff   Hard to bend, not easily bent—see Rigid.

Straight   Straight florets have no visible curvature throughout their entire length.

Strongly incurved   Vigorous, large proportion, decided upward curve in florets. Outer florets of a Pincer/Exhibition Cactus type toward the tip quickly curve forward toward the centre of the bloom.

Substance   Solidarity.

Symmetrical   Perfectly balanced in all respects, graceful and pleasing in appearance.

Texture   The almost invisible grain or ribs of a floret structure. Fine grain as of skin, painting etc. It includes the sparkle, sheen and brilliance of a plant and its blooms.

Tuber   The swollen root portion of a dahlia plant. The buds or ''eyes'' from which new plants are produced are on the crown, i.e. the base portion of the old plant's stalk near where the tuber is attached to it. The new plant is supplied with food from the tuber until fresh root growth takes over.

Tubular   Completely rounded as a tube or pipe, hollow stem. Note: the florets in the centre of an Anemone type dahlia are tubular.

Turn to one side   Growing to one or either side of the central direction, creating a whirling or revolving appearance. Note: Pincer/Exhibition Cactus type dahlias have florets which turn to one side.

Twisty   Turning to one side, turning around slightly.

Uniform   The same, consistent, conforming to a standard. Dahlia blooms which do not vary in form, size, colour or age.

Variety   A sub-group of a species eg. *Dahlia juraregili*, *Dahlia superflua* and *Dahlia variabilis*.

Viral disease/Virus   A plant disease spread by transfer of sap by cutting instruments or sucking insects. As there is no available cure infected plants should be immediately removed and burnt to protect healthy plants from it.

Wavy   Raising and lowering of the surface of florets along their length.

Wiring   An artificial aid to support weak stems. Weak stems are a serious fault and are heavily penalised. Furthermore, wiring could disqualify an exhibitor from entering in future shows.

Abbreviations

Pom	Pompon
L-Ball	Large Ball
S-Ball	Small Ball
G-FD	Giant Formal Decorative
L-FD	Large Formal Decorative
M-FD	Medium Formal Decorative
S-FD	Small Formal Decorative
MINI-FD	Miniature Formal Decorative
G-ID	Giant Informal Decorative
L-ID	Large Informal Decorative
M-ID	Medium Informal Decorative
S-ID	Small Informal Decorative
MINI-ID	Miniature Informal Decorative
G-SC	Giant Semi-cactus
L-SC	Large Semi-cactus
M-SC	Medium Semi-cactus
S-SC	Small Semi-cactus
MINI-SC	Miniature Semi-cactus
G-C	Giant Cactus
L-C	Large Cactus
M-C	Medium Cactus
S-C	Small Cactus
MINI-C	Miniature Cactus
L-PIN/L-EXC	Large Pincer/Exhibition Cactus
S-PIN/S-EXC	Small Pincer/Exhibition Cactus
L-FIM	Large Fimbriated
S-FIM	Small Fimbriated
ANE	Anemone
COLL	Collarette
NYM	Nymphea
ORCH	Orchid
STELL	Stellar
DIST	Distinct
C.V.A.	Colour Variation Allowed or Different Cultivars
N.A.S.	Not According to Schedule
N.N.D.	Not Necessarily Distinct
CULT	Cultivar
E	Exhibition Standard Cultivar
F	Floriferous, suitable for florists
G	Garden, suitable for display, but not indicative of exhibition standard.

Basic Show Schedule

Many of the present show schedules which include dahlia blooms, describe those blooms which may be exhibited in such a manner as to cause serious doubt as to the particular size and type of dahlia blooms required.

The two main objectives of a show schedule which contains classes for dahlia blooms should be:

1. To cater for all the recognised sizes and types of dahlias in order that each size and type is able to stand alone, free of the judge's preferences in this regard and to arouse public interest in them.

2. To provide a basis by which growers can enjoy a fair, just and comprehensive competition.

Prizes awarded at dahlia shows are usually of small value. Horticultural and dahlia societies are not in a financial position to spend large sums of money on prizes. Sponsorship is also very limited. This restriction of finances does, however, leave the simple pleasure of winning as a reward for effort. We have no desire to see a ''win at any cost'' attitude develop at our shows.

Show schedules should clearly and concisely describe the sizes and types of dahlias which may be entered in the classes. The following basic schedule is a minimum requirement. Classes for additional numbers of blooms should be added as required to satisfy the needs of the local exhibitors.

Standard Form Specimen Blooms

Grand Champion Bloom and Champion Bloom awards will be made for the best specimen bloom of each size and type of dahlia exhibited, if worthy.

Class	Description
1	3 blooms Large Ball N.N.D.
2	1 bloom Large Ball
3	3 blooms Small Ball N.N.D.
4	1 bloom Small Ball
5	3 blooms Pompon N.N.D.
6	1 bloom Pompon
7	3 blooms Giant Formal Decorative N.N.D.
8	1 bloom Giant Formal Decorative
9	3 blooms Large Formal Decorative N.N.D.
10	1 bloom Large Formal Decorative
11	3 blooms Medium Formal Decorative N.N.D.
12	1 bloom Medium Formal Decorative
13	3 blooms Small Formal Decorative N.N.D.
14	1 bloom Small Formal Decorative
15	3 blooms Miniature Formal Decorative N.N.D.
16	1 bloom Miniature Formal Decorative
17	3 blooms Giant Informal Decorative N.N.D.
18	1 bloom Giant Informal Decorative
19	3 blooms Large Informal Decorative N.N.D.
20	1 bloom Large Informal Decorative
21	3 blooms Medium Informal Decorative N.N.D.
22	1 bloom Medium Informal Decorative
23	3 blooms Small Informal Decorative N.N.D.
24	1 bloom Small Informal Decorative
25	3 blooms Miniature Informal Decorative N.N.D.
26	1 bloom Miniature Informal Decorative
27	3 blooms Giant Semi-cactus N.N.D.
28	1 bloom Giant Semi-cactus
29	3 blooms Large Semi-cactus N.N.D.
30	1 bloom Large Semi-cactus
31	3 blooms Medium Semi-cactus N.N.D.
32	1 bloom Medium Semi-cactus
33	3 blooms Small Semi-cactus N.N.D.
34	1 bloom Small Semi-cactus
35	3 blooms Miniature Semi-cactus N.N.D.
36	1 bloom Miniature Semi-cactus
37	3 blooms Giant Cactus N.N.D.
38	1 bloom Giant Cactus
39	3 blooms Large Cactus N.N.D.
40	1 bloom Large Cactus
41	3 blooms Medium Cactus N.N.D.
42	1 bloom Medium Cactus
43	3 blooms Small Cactus N.N.D.
44	1 bloom Small Cactus
45	3 blooms Miniature Cactus N.N.D.

Class	Description
46	1 bloom Miniature Cactus
47	3 blooms Large Pincer or Exhib. Cactus N.N.D.
48	1 bloom Large Pincer or Exhib. Cactus
49	3 blooms Small Pincer or Exhib. Cactus N.N.D.
50	1 bloom Small Pincer or Exhib. Cactus
51	3 blooms Large Fimbriated N.N.D.
52	1 bloom Large Fimbriated
53	3 blooms Small Fimbriated N.N.D.
54	1 bloom Small Fimbriated
55	3 blooms Nymphea N.N.D.
56	1 bloom Nymphea
57	3 blooms Collarette N.N.D.
58	1 bloom Collarette
59	3 blooms Anemone N.N.D.
60	1 bloom Anemone
61	3 blooms Orchid N.N.D.
62	1 bloom Orchid
63	3 blooms Stellar N.N.D.
64	1 bloom Stellar

Garden Display Blooms

Grand Premier Vase and Premier Vase awards will be made for the best vase of Garden Display blooms of each size group of blooms exhibited, if worthy.

Vases of 3 blooms of one cultivar in a vase.

Class	Description
65	3 vases of 3 blooms of one cultivar in a vase under 50 mm in diameter N.N.D.
66	1 vase of 3 blooms of one cultivar in a vase under 50 mm in diameter
67	3 vases of 3 blooms of one cultivar in a vase 50 to 120 mm in diameter N.N.D.
68	1 vase of 3 blooms of one cultivar in a vase 50 to 120 mm in diameter
69	3 vases of 3 blooms of one cultivar in a vase 120 to 160 mm in diameter N.N.D.
70	1 vase of 3 blooms of one cultivar in a vase 120 to 160 mm in diameter
71	3 vases of 3 blooms of one cultivar in a vase 160 to 210 mm in diameter N.N.D.
72	1 vase of 3 blooms of one cultivar in a vase 160 to 210 mm in diameter
73	3 vases of 3 blooms of one cultivar in a vase over 210 mm in diameter N.N.D.
74	1 vase of 3 blooms of one cultivar in a vase over 210 mm in diameter

Annual Cycle of Dahlia Growing

The end of the flowering season is the fulfilment of a dahlia plant's annual life cycle. The tubers which the plant has produced while flowering are the commencement of the next season's plant.

The clumps of tubers need to be dug, divided, legibly named and stored for next season. Once divided, the tubers can be named and stored in a bed of moist, coarse, washed sand, peatmoss, vermiculite, coarse pine sawdust, fine shellgrit or soil in a cool shed or similar place out of the direct sunshine and rain. Cover the tubers to a shallow depth. Dampen the bed after placing the tubers in it or a rack and keep it only just moist during the whole period of storage. This will keep the tubers plump and prevent them from shrivelling. Some tuber losses are inevitable but reasonable care will reduce your losses to a minimum. Naming is essential because a dahlia tuber or plant without a name is useless. Labels should also be placed to indicate where the cultivars are stored. However because these can be removed, even unintentionally, the tubers need to be named or at least coded with an indelible pencil or a water resistant black wick pen.

All old dahlia stalks, discarded tubers and other debris should be burnt or removed, not composted. This clearance of all dahlia waste material is necessary to prevent any possible spread of fungal diseases, which may be present in the dahlia patch.

When the dahlia beds have been cleared of last year's growth, the pH value of the soil should be checked. A pH reading of 6.5, slightly acid, is ideal for dahlia plants to obtain the nutrients they require from the soil. A reading of 5.5 would be ten times too acid. If the pH reading is below 6.5, garden lime should be applied to the soil after digging it in a rough state and allowed to weather in for about four or five weeks when the pH balance can again be checked. If the pH reading is above 6.5, agricultural sulphur can be applied and raked into the top soil to correct it. After four or five weeks, it can be tested again. Decayed pine bark, or acid leaf mould, dug in, will also correct an alkaline soil. Dressing of garden lime up to 225 gm per square metre or agricultural sulphur up to 30 gm per square metre can be applied according to the need.

A green crop of tick beans, field peas, lupins, rye corn, barley or oats should be sown as early as possible to ensure that it is sufficiently advanced and ready to turn into the soil together with a dressing of old farmyard manure, if necessary, at least six weeks prior to the proposed planting date. The crop should be either beginning to flower or form heads when turned into the soil. Don't allow it to mature or reach a rank state as much of its value will then be lost. If the soil is dry, water after digging the material into it because this will start the decaying action. If necessary, repeat the waterings.

If the soil needs fertilisers they can be added at the same time, but preferably apply them before the final digging and water the soil afterwards. Then after a few days, the patch will be ready for planting. If fertilisation is necessary at planting time either: place about 85 gm of the mixture in the planting hole and stir it into the soil below the tuber, or plant, and cover it with fresh soil to prevent immediate contact with the tuber or plant roots; or, after planting, place a band of the mixture 250 mm from the main stalk position and lightly hoe it into the soil. Always, the soil must be moist before applying fertilisers and watered immediately afterwards.

Clean all old labels and ensure that sufficient are on hand for the coming season. Pots should also be cleaned and seed can be planted early under glass or in beds in the open as soon as the danger of frost has passed.

Tubers need to be benched for the taking of cuttings for the coming season.

Pot tubers need to be repotted into fresh potting soil.

Transplant seedlings into small pots filled with potting mixture at a very eary stage. Harden them for at least two weeks before planting them into the open bed.

Ensure that your hot bed is working satisfactorily then commence taking cuttings. Strike them in a sterile, open mixture of soil and sand or either sand, vermiculite, perlite and peatmoss. Ensure that the cuttings are labelled immediately.

Keep abreast of preparation of your bed for planting later.

Commence potting your rooted cuttings as soon as possible after they start to grow into 100 mm to 125 mm pots filled with the potting mixture for green plants.

Guard the area against slugs and snails as they can do very serious damage to your dahlia plants. The damp, cool area between the pots is ideal for them to shelter.

After the final digging, stake the dahlia bed in readiness for planting. Plant seedlings, tubers or green plants into the open beds. Some tubers may have been left undisturbed where they grew last season for very early cut flowers. If the weather is dry, ensure that adequate water is supplied to the plants. To test the effectiveness of your watering, the day after watering, dig a shallow hole between the plants. Scoop up a handful of the lower soil and press it together tightly. If it has sufficient moisture, it will cling together in a ball. However, if it is too dry, it will crumble. When planting green plants into the open bed, the potting soil surrounding their roots should be washed away from them in a bucket full of water. Any curled roots may be straightened gently, under water. Plant the green plant in the required position, close to its stake and water it in with a copious quantity of water to settle the fresh soil around the roots of the plant.

Plantings for exhibition blooms should be carried out sufficiently early to allow the plants to grow and produce flowers for the shows. Any replacements required, and there usually are several, should be made as soon as it is realised that the original plant has failed to grow. Three weeks is the maximum time a tuber should take to grow its shoot through the soil, so all replacements should be completed by then. Water the dahlia patch regularly from the time of planting in the absence of sufficient rain to ensure that the young tubers and plants are kept growing. It is wrong to plant then hold the plants back from growing. Hoe the bed fortnightly to eradicate weeds and aerate the soil.

Tie your plants when they reach about 100 mm in height; a tie at this stage will encourage them to grow. Keep tying as necessary, remembering to check that stalk growth has not tightened the ties sufficiently to prevent the sap from flowing freely. If a tie is too tight, cut or remove it, and replace if necessary with another tie. Stop all plants as required. Follow up with the removal of lateral growths which are to be discarded as soon as you are able to handle them.

The number of laterals and/or water shoots allowed to continue growing should be in accordance with the cultivar and the size of the flowers the plant is to produce. The smaller the flower size, the greater the number of laterals which may be allowed to flower. Don't discard watershoots as they will produce better blooms.

Wash off your plants with a fine spray of water morning and evening during very hot weather. Water on the foliage of dahlias does not cause burning, but salt or other chemicals dissolved in it may do considerable damage.

Wind can cause much havoc amongst your dahlia plants so ensure that they are kept tied securely to stakes.

Fertiliser and/or farmyard manure mulches should be applied to the dahlia patch, as required, after the sixth week of growth when the first buds are forming. The soil should be moist when these are applied and watered copiously immediately afterwards.

Remove and burn any plants which are infected with viral diseases, replacing them with healthy plants if available.

Watering should be gradually increased and maintained during the flowering season as the plants are larger and producing flowers and tubers from now until the end of their flowering season.

Continue to disbud the plants about twice weekly to obtain the best flowers possible.

If the blooms are required for exhibition, cover the buds to protect them from dew and excessive sunshine when colour begins to show as the first two rows of florets open.

Plant any green plants left over after filling the beds. These will provide stock of small clumps of tubers for next season, which are ideal for despatching to distant destinations.

Clean glasshouse or glass frame and storage beds or racks and burn any pieces of dahlia tubers or plants which may have been surplus to your requirements or have failed to grow. Ensure that the sand or other material used to cover the tubers is clean. Replace any which has had rotten tubers in it with fresh supplies. Clean pots and disinfect them in readiness for next season's plantings.

Take any latecuttings from near the base of flowering plants, strike them and keep them growing with bottom heat for as long as possible into the winter. Provided they make fibrous roots, they will probably regrow in the spring. See section on latecuttings for full details on stock plants. Keep a check upon your plants to ensure that they are tied securely. Examine your flowers that are opening as often as time permits and remove any malformed florets during this time.

Pick and scald the ends of stems of flowers required for exhibition the evening before the show. Place the blooms in a cool well-protected area in deep containers with plenty of water to condition them.

Cover flowers which you need for hand pollination. Carefully make the crossings desired and keep a record of your work for future reference. The results must also be recorded when known.

Keep the soil moist during this critical stage of the plant's life. The plants are flowering and forming tubers for next season.

Follow up with a further application of fertiliser four weeks after the earlier, first bud stage application. Only apply this additional fertiliser if needed and if there is time for the plants to benefit from it before the close of the season. Applications of fertiliser should always be made when the soil is moist and followed up with a heavy watering immediately afterwards.

Remove all unwanted blooms which have passed their prime. Burn or otherwise dispose of them as their deteriorating condition is ideal for harbouring fungal diseases.

Allow mature flowers required for seed to remain on the plants. Carefully pluck the dying florets from the seed pods.

Gradually reduce watering according to weather conditions.

Gather, clean, dry and store seed for next season.

When the plants have finished flowering, the clumps may be lifted, divided and stored for the next season. There is no reason to wait until the plants have died back, in fact, early lifting and storage is beneficial in combatting fungal diseases.

Recommended Cultivars

These cultivars have been listed under the various sizes and types of dahlias to assist exhibitors when choosing their collections. However, the dahlia is a delicate flower and its florets will change in their form under slightly different climatic, soil or cultivation conditions. Therefore, in your garden, they may belong to a neighbouring group. This applies more particularly to the Formal Decorative, Informal Decorative, Semi-cactus and Cactus types. The numbers are colour plates.

Large Ball

Name	Colour
'Bloodhound'	Dark red
'Brant'	Smokey pink with cream base
'Brookside Snowball'	White
'Christie Miss'	Mauve with deeper mauve reverse
'George Tucker'	Dark red
'L'Ancresse' (2)	White with faint lavender flush
'Purple Globe'	Purple
'Red Admiral' (9)	Red
'Risca Miner' (1)	Purple
'Snoho Tammie'	Pale lavender with white base
'Queen of Spades'	Purple
'Wootton Cupid'	Lavender pink

Small Ball

'Alltami Cherrie' (7)	Dark red
'Bitsa' (6)	Dark red
'Bullseye'	Bright red
'Nettie'	Yellow
'Nijinski'	Deep lavender
'Sea Kiss' (8)	Pale lavender
'Vaguely Noble'	Purple
'White Nettie' (10)	White

Pompon

'Buttercup' (13)	Yellow
'Hallmark'	Pink
'Linda Harris'	Pink
'Little Sally'	Bright red
'Little Snowdrop' (14)	White
'Magnificent'	Red
'Moore Place'	Purple

Name	Colour
'Mrs Black'	Yellow
'Pam'	Pink
'Little Pearl'	Lavender pink
'Pop Willo' (15)	Gold
'Small World'	White
'Stoneleigh Joyce'	Red
'White Pam'	Palest pink
'Willo's Surprise'	Purple red

Orchid

'Ada Hardisty'	Yellow with cyclamen reverse
'Koala' (16)	Gold with reddish maroon reverse

Stellar

'Acacia Julie' (24)	Mauve pink with deeper mauve pink reverse
'Acacia Pink'	Salmon pink with deeper salmon pink reverse
'Acacia Yellow'	Golden yellow with trace of red on reverse
'Christie Jess' (22)	Lavender with deeper lavender reverse
'Jescot Julie' (23)	Gold with reddish reverse

Nymphea

'Brunell' (30)	Honey gold
'Cameo' (27)	Cream
'Fern Irene'	Yellow
'Figurine' (26)	Shell pink with cream base
'Hiawatha'	Bright orange with yellow base
'Lady's Choice'	Pale Pink
'Landis' (28)	Red with yellow base
'Muriel Fern'	Bright orange with bright yellow base
'Red Velvet' (29)	Dark red with cream base

Giant Formal Decorative

'Arthur Hambly'	Mauve pink
'Corio'	Golden salmon
'Edge of Gold' (31)	Pink with gold tips

Name	Colour
'Helen West'	Mauve pink
'Louisa Rossack' (33)	Lilac
'Polyanna'	Lavender

Large Formal Decorative
Name	Colour
'Alabaster Queen'	White
'Colac'	Bronzed with gold tips
'Como Perfection'	Lavender with white base
'Croydon Snotop'	White
'Dad's Day' (34)	Salmon pink
'Doris Day'	Apricot
'Formby Queen'	White
'Ronlea Martin'	Deep lavender
'Santa Anita' (35)	Salmon pink
'Springfield Lavender' (32)	Lavender 'Bonaventure'
'Terry Cook'	Bright yellow

Medium Formal Decorative
Name	Colour
'Cyclamen Don'	Cyclamen pink
'Dreamland'	White with soft lavender flush
'First Lady'	Pale yellow
'Formby Royal'	Dark Red
'Maggie Hannaford' (36)	White with cyclamen flush
'Purple Joy' (40)	Purple
'Sherwood Standard'	Gold
'Thebarton'	Lavender with white base

Small Formal Decorative
Name	Colour
'Frank Hornsey' (45)	Pale orange with yellow centre
'Jeanie'	Bright gold with coppery red flush
'Lady Linda'	Yellow
'Linda May'	Creamy white
'Mary'	White with cyclamen flush
'Muir's Choice'	Salmon pink with yellow base
'Nationwide'	Autumn tones
'Pink Frank Hornsey' (44)	Lavender pink with cream base
'Simplicious'	Deep lavender
'Suffolk Hero' (46)	Cream
'Torquay'	Purple
'White Hornsey'	White
'Yellow Hornsey'	Yellow

Miniature Formal Decorative
Name	Colour
'Bracken Buttercup'	Cream
'Bracken Rocket'	Dark rose pink

Name	Colour
'Bracken Blush'	White with pale lavender flush
'Eastwin' (48)	Pink
'Formby Opal'	Smoky mauve pink with gold tips
'Glacier' (47)	White
'Kosi Snowball'	White
'Sally Ann' (49)	Cream
'Sandra' (50)	Deep salmon pink

Giant Informal Decorative
Name	Colour
'Amelia's Surprise'	Mauve with white base
'Barbara Schnell'	Salmon bronze
'Barney Flowers'	Creamy yellow
'Bon Adventure'	Bright gold
'Brenton Sellick' (55)	Dark red
'Carolyn Fay'	Rusty red
'Croydon Jumbo'	Pale salmon pink
'Croydon Superior' (56)	Salmon pink
'Evelyn Rumbold' (53)	Purple
'Hamari Girl'	Lavender pink
'Hamari Gold'	Golden bronze
'Thelma Davidson'	Cream with lavender pink flush
'The Master' (51)	Golden bronze

Large Informal Decorative
Name	Colour
'Alden Super'	Lilac with paler base
'Almand's Climax' (60)	Lavender with white base
'Alva's Supreme'	Yellow
'Amazing Grace'	Salmon pink
'Barbara Elaine' (57)	Orange bronze
'Croydon Amber'	Salmon amber
'Croydon Apricot'	Apricot gold
'Croydon Twilight'	Golden bronze
'Doris Fay'	Apricot
'Formby Supreme' (61)	Bright yellow
'Kidd's Climax' (59)	Pink with cream base
'Madeline Ann' (58)	Golden yellow
'Murray Serene'	Pastel pink with white base
'Formby Marvel'	White

Medium Informal Decorative
Name	Colour
'Edna C.' (63)	Pale yellow
'Evelyn Foster'	White
'Gilt Edge' (62)	Mauve pink tipped gold
'Gay Glory'	Dark red
'Gold Coast' (65)	Orange gold with yellow at base
'Mrs A. Woods' (64)	Deep lavender
'Reta Easterbrook'	Dark red
'Rustig'	Cream

Name	Colour
'Ted's Icecap'	White
'White Rustig'	White

Small Informal Decorative
Name	Colour
'Ann's Delight' (67)	Pale lavender with white base
'Jimmy Meredith' (66)	Creamy white
'Little Sister'	Yellow heavily tipped white
'Margaret Eleanor'	Yellow

Miniature Informal Decorative
Name	Colour
'Bracken Aurora'	Cream
'Christie Red' (69)	Red
'Dr Tanner'	Red
'Josh'	Lavender

Giant Semi-cactus
Name	Colour
'Alfred C'	Orange gold
'Bramley's Sunset'	Red with gold markings
'Conquistadore'	Orange
'Florence Baker' (75)	White
'Gay Triumph' (74)	Pale orange gold
'Inca Dambuster'	Cream
'Maxmann' (71)	Red with gold tips
'St Joan' (72)	White
'Sunrise'	Yellow

Large Semi-cactus
Name	Colour
'Agricola'	Dark autumn tones
'Candy Keene' (78)	Lavender pink with white centre
'Gay Beauty' (76)	American Beauty pink
'Gay Gertie' (77)	Golden bronze
'Gretta'	Pale autumn tints
'Kingdown Leader'	Dark salmon gold
'Neveric'	Orange gold
'Reginald Keene' (79)	Orange gold with yellow centre
'Robbie Huston'	Purple
'Salmon Keene'	Salmon pink to gold
'Suffolk Conquest'	White faintly flushed lavender
'Vidale Rhapsody'	Pale lavender with white centre

Medium Semi-cactus
Name	Colour
'Autumn Fire'	Deep amber
'Bob's Gold' (83)	Orange gold
'Brighton Amber'	Amber
'Eastwood Pinky'	Lavender pink with white centre
'Formby Sparkle' (85)	Bright yellow
'Gay Chieftain'	Red
'Gay Peach'	Peach with cream base

Name	Colour
'Gay Pride' (81)	Cream
'Gay Sunset' (cover)	Salmon orange with creamy yellow centre
'Hamari Caprice'	Cream with pastel pink flush
'Lavender Gay' (84)	Lavender with paler centre
'Silver Gay' (82)	White

Small Semi-cactus
Name	Colour
'Davenport Sunlight'	Bright yellow
'Dr J. Fisher'	White
'Gay's Choice' (89)	Cream with pink flush
'Gay Delight' (86)	Cream with dark pink flush
'Gay Master' (88)	Golden bronze
'Gay Snowflake'	White
'Gay Queen'	Purple
'Kiwi Brother'	Dark salmon pink
'Sharrowean Pride'	Cream with mauve pink flush

Miniature Semi-cactus
Name	Colour
'Alma Dryden'	Lavender purple
'Brian's First' (94)	Pale mauve pink with creamy centre
'Elaine Gay' (91)	Cerise
'Gay Faye'	Cream heavily flushed dark salmon pink
'Gay Prince' (93)	Dark Red
'Jean' (92)	Gold with cream base
'Jean Wanless'	Dark pink with mauve sheen
'Leslie'	Deep lavender
'Match' (95)	White with cerise flush
'Polly'	Lavender
'Rufus'	Brick red
'Twinkletoes'	White heavily tipped cyclamen pink

Giant Cactus
Name	Colour
'Alden Imperial' (97)	Pale lavender pink with cream centre
'Alden Joy' (98)	Orange yellow
'Daleko Jupiter' (100)	Orange with gold base
'Kwinana Joy'	Bright pink
'Lavender Lodge'	Palest lavender
'Pink Jupiter'	Lavender with white centre
'Pooraka Snowstorm' (96)	White

Large Cactus
Name	Colour
'Comment' (101)	White with pale pink flush

Name	Colour
'Como Reliable'	White
'Como Tresbon' (105)	Pastel pink
'Daisy Becker'	Cream with pale pink flush
'Gambier Jewel' (103)	Mauve pink
'Gay Sweetheart'	Lavender pink
'Golden Planet' (102)	Golden yellow
'Hamari Katrina' (104)	Cream
'Hamari Sunset'	Autumn shades
'Ruby Wilson'	Dark purplish red
'Sara G.'	Salmon pink with yellow centre
'Satellite'	White

Medium Cactus

Name	Colour
'Daleko Venus' (109)	Cyclamen pink
'Formby Debutante'	Bright lolly pink
'Formby Romance'	Golden yellow
'Heather' (110)	White
'Janet Gay'	Dark salmon pink
'Jan Lennon' (106)	White flushed pale pink
'Jan-the-Second'	White flushed pink
'Margery Wilson'	Creamy white flushed mauve pink
'Neva Ray'	Lavender with white base
'Pretty Girl'	White faintly flushed pink
'Suffolk Bride'	White
'Sunset' (108)	Yellow with red flush
'Susan French' (107)	Mauve pink with light centre

Small Cactus

Name	Colour
'Barbara Kappler' (113)	Lavender pink with white centre
'Brighton Bronze'	Golden bronze
'Brighton Joy'	Red with yellow base
'Carol's Choice'	Pale salmon pink with yellow centre
'Desert Lodge' (111)	Salmon pink
'Formby Blaze'	Dark red
'Formby Venus'	Yellow
'Gambier Champagne'	Pale orange bronze
'Gay Snowdrop' (112)	White
'Gilda'	Pale yellow
'Goodwill'	Lavender pink
'Karen Joy'	Golden yellow
'Pink Desert Lodge'	Deep salmon pink
'Reform'	Bright red
'Sharon Gay' (115)	White
'Sierra'	Golden yellow
'Trixie Telford'	Pale bronze
'Valetta'	White flushed mauve
'4XXXX'	Mauve pink

Name	Colour
Miniature Cactus	
'Alden Dainty'	Pale mauve pink
'Alden Snowlodge' (118)	White
'Debutante' (117)	Mauve pink
'Dianne McKenzie'	White tipped cyclamen
'Dusky Maid'	Pale salmon pink
'Grace Candy' (116)	White
'Jill's Red'	Rusty red with gold base
'Judith Candy'	Deep salmon pink
'Little Glen Fern'	Cream
'Margaret'	White tipped cyclamen
'Mrs J. Robertson'	Pale mauve pink with white centre
'Red Regal' (119)	Red tipped gold
'Rosie'	White flush lavender
'Sue Ann'	Pale mauve pink with cream centre
'Wee Willie'	Mauve pink with cream base
'White Robbie'	White

Large Pincer/Exhibition Cactus

Name	Colour
'Ballerina' (123)	Lavender pink
'Carlisle Gold'	Golden yellow
'Cricket' (122)	White with lilac flush
'Freelancer' (121)	Cream with pale salmon flush
'Gwen's Choice' (124)	Yellow
'Mayarin'	Golden bronze
'Mayday'	White
'Mettie'	Pale golden bronze

Small Pincer/Exhibition Cactus

Name	Colour
'Joan'	Deep lavender purple
'Jo Jo' (134)	Gold
'Winsome'	Pale pink shades

Large Fimbriated

Name	Colour
'Adeline'	Pale mauve pink with paler centre
'Frontispiece' (130)	Pale cream
'Gambier's Best'	White
'International' (126)	Creamy white
'Jennifer Toombe'	Lavender with white base
'Landmarker'	Red
'Pyjama Game'	White with mauve pink flush

Small Fimbriated

Name	Colour
'Apache' (133)	Red
'Miss A.'	Golden bronze
'Pink Lace' (131)	Pink with white base

Name	Colour
Collarette	
'Beckie'	Pale pink/white collar
'Bushfire' (142)	Dark red/cream collar
'Fascination'	Purple tipped white/white collar
'Festival'	White heavily flushed carmine/white collar
'Limit' (140)	Cerise tipped white/cream collar
'Peace'	Plum purple/white collar
'Trevor'	Deep magenta tipped white/white collar
Anemone	
'Comet' (136)	Dark red
'Fabel' (137)	Bright red
'Grisby' (138)	Bright yellow
'Honey' (139)	Soft gold shades
Garden Display Blooms	
'Brookside Snowball'	L.Ball—White
'Eureka'	L.Ball—Cream heavily flushed maroon
'Silver Tips'	POM—Lavender edged white
'Willo Cooee'	POM—Mauve pink
'Helena'	SID—Purple flushed white
'Little Sister'	SID—Yellow flushed white
'Christine Hammett'	MINI FD—Cream

Name	Colour
'Gambier Jane'	MINI FD—White flushed purple
'Mollie's Delight'	MINI FD—Pink
'Libby's Choice' (144)	MSC—Yellow flushed red
'Bertie Bromley' (148)	SC—Yellow flushed red
'Callum's Choice'	SC—White tipped pink
'Freda's Choice'	SC—White tipped cyclamen
'Gay Sunrise'	SC—Autumn shades
'Hayley Jane'	SC—White tipped deep cyclamen
'Maureen Quigley' (146)	SC—Pale lavender pink
'Mrs A.F. Rees'	SC—Dark red
'Oriental' (147)	SC—Autumn shades
'Glen Bank Twinkle'	MINI C—White tipped deep lavender
'Night Life'	MINI C—Red tipped gold
'Twinkletoes'	MINI C—White tipped cyclamen
'Eddie Howard'	L.PIN/EX.C.—Pink
'Joanne Heron'	L.PIN/EX.C.—Pale pink

These Garden Display cultivars are a few of the attractive ones which add colour to the garden. There are a number of others. Also many of the cutivars mentioned under their sizes and types are prolific flowering and can be used for garden display purposes.

Index

References are page numbers and plate numbers in brackets.

Abbreviations, 68
Acidity, 15, 71
Aeration, 37
Agricultural Sulphur, 15, 71
Alkaline, 15, 71
American Dahlia Society, 4
Anemone type, 7, 30, 42, 61, 63, 70, 78
  'Comet', 30, 78, (136)
  'Fabel', 30, 78, (137)
  'Grisby', 30, 78, (138)
  'Honey', 30, 78, (139)
Angle of Flowers, 43, 58
Animal Manure, 12, 15-6, 39, 71
Annual conferences, 13, 62
Assessment, 59, 60-5
Australian Dahlia Council, 4, 13, 59, 60, 62-5

Australian Guide, 62
Bamboo, 33, 43, 57
Ball type, 17, 42-3, 60, 62, 69, 74
  Large:
  'Asana Yama', 17, (5)
  'Bloodhound', 74
  'Brant', 74
  'Brookside Snowball', 74
  'Christie Miss', 74
  'Eureka', 78
  'George Tucker', 74
  'Kent', 17, (4)
  'L'Ancresse', 17, 74, (2)
  'Mrs Brown', 17, (3)
  'Purple Globe', 74
  'Red Admiral', 17, 74, (9)
  'Risca Miner', 17, 74, (1)
  'Snoho Tammie', 74
  'Queen of Spades', 74

  'Wooton Cupid', 74
  Small:
  'Alltami Cherrie', 17, 74, (7)
  'Bitsa', 17, 74, (6)
  'Bullseye', 74
  'Nettie', 74
  'Nijinski', 74
  'Sea Kiss', 17, 74, (8)
  'Vaguely Noble', 74
  'White Nettie', 17, 74, (10)
Basic Show Schedule, 69
Bedding Dahlias, 6, 54
Blooms, 6-9, 12-7, 33, 36, 38, 40-7, 49, 51-5, 56-9, 62-4, 69, 71-3
Buds, 9, 13, 37-9, 42, 44-6, 48-9, 54, 57-8, 72
Cactus type, 7, 26-8, 42, 46, 61, 63, 69, 74, 76-7

Giant:
  'Alden Imperial', 26, 76, (97)
  'Alden Joy', 26, 76, (98)
  'Daleko Jupiter', 26, 76, (100)
  'Griffin's Pride', 26, (99)
  'Kwinana Joy' 76
  'Lavender Lodge', 76
  'Pink Jupiter', 76
  'Pooraka Snowstorm', 26, 76, (96)
  Large:
  'Comment', 27, 76, (101)
  'Como Reliable', 77
  'Como Tresbon', 27, 77, (105)
  'Daisy Becker', 77
  'Gambier Jewel', 27, 77, (103)
  'Gay Sweetheart', 77
  'Golden Planet', 27, 77, (102)
  'Hamari Katrina', 27, 77, (104)

'Hamari Sunset', 77
'Ruby Wilson', 77
'Sara G.' 77
'Satellite', 77
Medium:
'Daleko Venus', 27, 77, (109)
'Formby Debutante', 77
'Formby Romance', 77
'Gambier Princess', 31, 78, (145)
'Heather', 27, 77, (110)
'Janet Gay', 77
'Jan Lennon', 27, 77, (106)
'Jan-the-Second', 77
'Margery Wilson', 77
'Neva Ray', 77
'Pretty Girl', 77
'Suffolk Bride', 77
'Sunset', 27, 77, (108)
'Susan French', 27, 77, (107)
Small:
'Barbara Kappler', 28, 77, (113)
'Bertie Bromley', 28, 31, 77, 78, (114)
'Brighton Bronze', 77
'Brighton Joy', 77
'Callum's Choice', 78
'Carol's Choice', 77
'Desert Lodge', 28, 77, (111)
'Formby Blaze', 77
'Formby Venus', 77
'Freda's Choice', 78
'Gambier Champagne', 77
'Gay Snowdrop', 28, 77, (112)
'Gay Sunrise', 78
'Gilda', 77
'Goodwill', 77
'Hayley Jane', 78
'Karen Joy', 77
'Maureen Quigley', 31, 78, (146)
'Mrs A.F. Rees', 78
'Oriental', 31, 78, (147)
'Pink Desert Lodge', 77
'Reform', 77
'Sharon Gay', 28, 77, (115)
'Sierra', 77
'Trixie Telford', 77
'Valetta', 77
'4XXXX', 77
Miniature:
'Alden Dainty', 77
'Alden Snowlodge', 28, 77, (118)
'Debutante', 28, 77, (117)
'Dianne McKenzie', 77
'Dusky Maid', 77
'Glenbank Twinkle', 78
'Grace Candy', 28, 77, (116)
'Jill's Red', 77
'Judith Candy', 77
'Little Glen Fern', 77
'Margaret', 77
'Milford', 28, 77, (120)
'Mrs J. Robertson', 77
'Night Life', 78
'Red Regal', 28, 77, (119)
'Rosie', 77
'Sue Ann', 77
'Twinkletoes', 78
'Wee Willie', 77
'White Robbie', 77
Calyx, 43
Canes, 33, 43
Centre, 7, 52-3, 57, 60-3
Characteristics, 6-7, 17-32, 48-51, 54, 58-65
Charm dahlias, 7

Chemicals, 10, 36-7, 55, 72
Classes, 57, 69, 70
Classification, 62
Clumps, 8, 14-5, 34, 71, 73
Cold storage, 52
Collarette type, 6, 7, 31, 52, 61, 63, 70, 78
'Beckie', 78
'Bushfire', 31, 78, (142)
'Clem's Yellow', 31, (141)
'Fascination', 78
'Festival', 78
'Hades', 31, 78, (143)
'Limit', 31, 78, (140)
'Peace', 78
'Trevor', 78
Collections, 6, 54, 74-8
Colour 6, 14, 33, 38, 46-7, 49, 51, 54, 56, 58-9, 64, 78
Compost, 15, 55, 71
Condition, 6, 11, 13-5, 33, 36, 38, 46-7, 48-9, 53, 57-9, 64, 74
Conferences, 13, 62
Copper sulphate, 38-9
C.S.I.R.O., 4, 15
Cultivars, 6-8, 10-4, 34, 40-4, 46, 48-9, 51-2, 59, 62, 71-2, 74-8
Cultivation, 10, 33, 49, 55, 59, 74
Cut flowers, 6, 33, 52, 57, 62
Cuttings, 9, 10-14, 34, 48-9, 71
Daylight, 13, 41, 52
Decoration, 6, 33, 48
Decorative type, 7, 14, 20-3, 42, 74
see Formal and Informal Decorative types
Disbudding, 42-3, 49, 50, 58, 72
Disease, 55-6, 71, 73
Distinguishing characteristics, 6-7, 17-32, 48-51, 54, 58-65
Dividing clumps, 8, 34, 71
Dormancy, 13, 53
Drainage, 10, 12, 15, 35, 49, 50, 54
Drawing attention, 59
Drooping, 35-6
Dwarf Bedding, 6, 54
Epsom salts, 38
Evaluation, 59-65
Exhibition Cactus type, 29-30, 61, 63, 70, 77
Large:
'Ballerina', 29, 77, (123)
'Carlisle Gold', 77
'Cricket', 29, 77, (122)
'Eddie Howard', 78
'Freelancer', 29, 77, (121)
'Gloaming', 29, (125)
'Gwen's Choice', 29, 77, (124)
'Joanne Heron', 78
'Mayarin', 77
'Mayday', 77
'Mettie', 77
Small:
'Joan', 77
'Jo Jo', 30, 77, (134)
'Town Topic', 30, 77, (135)
'Winsome', 77
Exhibiting, 6, 11, 44, 48, 54, 57-8, 62-5, 69-70, 72
Exhibitors, 7, 47, 54, 57, 59, 69, 74
Farmyard manure, 12, 15-6, 38-9, 49, 71-2

Fertilise, 52
Fertiliser, 11-2, 15-6, 38-9, 48-9, 50, 52, 56, 71-3
Fimbriated type, 29-30, 61, 63, 70, 77
Large:
'Adeline', 77
'Frontispiece', 29, 77, (130)
'Gambier's Best', 77
'Helen Louise', 29, 77, (129)
'International', 29, 77, (126)
'Jennifer Toombe', 77
'Landmarker', 77
'Pyjama Game', 77
'Show-N-Tell', 29, 77, (127)
'Wavabeauta', 29, 77, (128)
Small:
'Apache', 30, 77, (133)
'Fresco', 30, 77, (132)
'Miss A.', 77
'Pink Lace', 30, 77, (131)
Florets/petals, 6, 7, 38, 43, 46-7, 51-3, 57, 59, 60-4, 72-3
Flowers/blooms, 6-9, 12-7, 33, 36, 38, 40-7, 49, 51-5, 56-9, 62-4, 71-3
Flower Pot Dahlias, 11, 13, 48-9, 50, 58
Form, 6, 7, 33, 51, 59-64, 69
Formal Decorative type, 7, 14, 20-1, 42, 60, 62, 69, 74-5
Giant:
'Arthur Hambly', 74
'Corio', 74
'Edge of Gold', 20, 74, (31)
'Helen West', 75
'Louisa Rossack', 20, 75, (33)
'Polyanna', 75
Large:
'Alabaster Queen', 75
'Colac', 75
'Como Perfection', 75
'Croydon Snotop', 75
'Dad's Day', 20, 75, (34)
'Doris Day', 75
'Formby Queen', 75
'Ronlea Martin', 75
'Santa Anita', 20, 75, (35)
'Springfield Lavender', 20, 75, (32)
'Terry Cook', 75
Medium:
'Alloway Cottage', 20, (37)
'Bob Stanners', 20, (38)
'Cyclamen Don', 75
'Dreamland', 75
'First Lady', 75
'Formby Lavender', 20, (39)
'Formby Royal', 75
'Maggie Hannaford', 20, 75, (36)
'Purple Joy', 20, 75, (40)
'Sherwood Standard', 75
'Thebarton', 75
Small:
'Alden Blue Hills', 21, (43)
'Formby Gem', 21, (41)
'Frank Hornsey', 21, 75, (45)
'Jeanie', 21
'Lady Linda', 75
'Linda May', 75
'Mary', 75
'George Matherson', 21, (42)
'Muir's Choice', 75
'Nationwide', 75
'Pink Frank Hornsey', 21, 75, (44)
'Simplicious', 75
'Suffolk Hero', 21, 75, (46)

'Torquay', 75
'White Hornsey', 75
'Yellow Hornsey', 75
Miniature:
'Bracken Buttercup', 75
'Bracken Rocket', 75
'Bracken Blush', 75
'Eastwin', 21, 75, , (48)
'Formby Opal', 75
'Gambier Jane', 78
'Glacier', 21, 75, (47)
'Kosi Snowball', 75
'Mollie's Delight', 78
'Sally Ann', 21, 75, (49)
'Sandra', 21, 75, (50)
Frost, 8, 9, 54, 71
Fungal disease, 43, 50, 53, 55, 71, 73
Garden Display, 6, 11, 31, 48, 54, 59, 70, 78
'Bertie Bromley', 31, 78, (148)
'Brookside Snowball', 78
'Callum's Choice', 78
'Christine Hammett', 78
'Eddie Howard', 78
'Eureka', 78
'Freda's Choice', 78
'Gambier Jane', 78
'Gambier Princess', 31, (145)
'Gay Sunrise', 78
'Glenbank Twinkle', 78
'Hayley Jane', 78
'Helena', 78
'Joanne Heron', 78
'Libby's Choice', 31, 78, (144)
'Little Sister', 78
'Maureen Quigley', 31, 78, (146)
'Mollie's Delight', 78
'Mrs A.F. Rees', 78
'Night Life', 78
'Oriental', 31, 78, (147)
'Silver Tips', 78
'Twinkletoes', 78
'Willo Cooee', 78
Giant *see* Cactus, Formal Decorative, Informal Decorative and Semi-cactus types
Glass frame, 9, 10, 72
Glasshouse, 9, 10, 13, 72
Glossary of terms, 66
Green crop, 15, 16, 38, 71
Green plants, 6, 9-12, 14, 34, 40, 48-50, 54, 71-2
Hardening off, 11, 12, 14, 34, 54, 71
Hard-wooded, 10, 40, 44
Heat, 9, 11, 13, 54, 71
Herbs, 55
History, 7
Hoeing, 5, 37, 71-2
Holding attention, 59
Hormone, 10
Hot bed, 9-11, 13, 54, 71
Humidity, 10, 13, 36, 54
Hybrids, 7, 51
Informal Decorative type, 7, 14, 22-3, 42, 60-3, 69, 74, 76
Giant:
'Amelia's Surprise', 75
'Barbara Schnell', 75
'Barney Flowers', 75
'Bonaventure', 75
'Brenton Sellick', 22, 75, (55)
'Carolyn Fay', 75
'Croydon Jumbo', 75
'Croydon Superior', 22, 75, (56)

'Evelyn Rumbold', 22, 75, (53)
'Hamari Girl', 75
'Hamari Gold', 75
'Lena Lila', 22, (52)
'My Doris', 22, (52)
'Thelma Davidson', 75
'The Master', 22, 75, (51)
Large:
'Alden Super', 75
'Almand's Climax', 22, 75, (60)
'Alva's Supreme', 75
'Amazing Grace', 75
'Barbara Elaine', 22, 75, (57)
'Croydon Amber', 75
'Croydon Apricot', 75
'Croydon Twilight', 75
'Doris Fay', 75
'Formby Supreme', 23, 75, (61)
'Kidd's Climax', 22, 75, (59)
'Madeline Ann', 22, 75, (58)
'Murray Serene', 75
'Formby Marvel', 75
Medium:
'Edna C', 23, 75, (63)
'Evelyn Foster', 75
'Gilt Edge', 23, 75, (62)
'Gay Glory', 75
'Gold Coast', 23, 75, (65)
'Mrs A. Woods', 23, 75, (64)
'Reta Easterbrook', 75
'Rustig', 75
'Ted's Icecap', 76
'White Rustig', 76
Small:
'Ann's Delight', 23, 76, (67)
'Christine Hammett', 78
'Helena', 78
'Jimmy Meredith', 23, 76, (66)
'Little Sister', 76, 78
'Margaret Eleanor', 76
'Wonder City', 23, (68)
Miniature:
'Bracken Aurora', 76
'Christie Red', 23, 76, (69)
'Dr Tanner', 76
'Josh', 76
'Shirley Pride', 23, (70)
Insects, 36, 51-2, 55
Iron sulphate, 38-9
Labels, 10, 14, 52, 54, 71
Latecuttings, 11-3, 48-9, 50, 72
Lateral, 12, 34, 41-2, 44-5, 48-9, 58, 72
Leaf joint node, 10, 12-13, 40, 42-4, 49
Leaf mould, 12, 71
Lifting tubers, 8, 51, 73
Light, 9, 13, 37
Lime, 15-6, 71
Lime sulphur, 55
Liquid fertiliser, 12, 39, 50
Liquid manure, 12, 39, 48-9, 71
Magnesium sulphate, 38-9
Manure, 12, 15-6, 38-9, 48-9, 55
Mulch, 36-7, 72
Name, 8, 10, 12, 14, 58, 71
Neck, 8, 51
Neck stretcher, 43, 58
Nitrogen, 15, 38-9
Node, 9, 10, 12-3, 33, 40, 43-4, 49

Nymphea type, 7, 19, 60, 63, 70, 74
'Brunell', 19, 74, (30)
'Cameo', 19, 74, (27)
'Fern Irene', 74
'Figurine', 19, 74, (26)
'Hiawatha', 74
'Lady's Choice', 74
'Landis', 19, 74, (28)
'Muriel Fern', 74
'Red Velvet', 19, 74, (29)
Orchid type, 7, 18, 42, 52, 60, 63, 70, 74
'Ada Hardisty', 74
'Koala', 18, 74, (16)
'Pink Orchid', 18, (17)
'Seattle Star', 18, (18)
Peat Moss, 11, 54
Peony type, 7
Pests, 36, 55, 72
Petal/floret, 6, 7, 38, 43, 46-7, 51-3, 57, 59, 60-4, 72-3
PH Balance, 12, 15, 71
Phosphorus, 38-9
Picking flowers, 42-3, 49, 57, 72
Pincer type, 29, 30, 61, 63, 70, 77
Large:
'Ballerina', 29, 77, (123)
'Carlisle Gold', 77
'Cricket', 29, 77, (122)
'Eddie Howard', 78
'Freelancer', 29, 77, (121)
'Gloaming', 29, (125)
'Gwen's Choice', 29, 77, (124)
'Joanne Heron', 78
'Mayarin', 77
'Mayday', 77
'Mettie', 77
Small:
'Joan', 77
'Jo Jo', 30, 77, (134)
'Town Topic', 30, (135)
'Winsome', 77
Plant food deficiencies, 39
Planting, 9-16, 33-4, 39, 48, 54, 71-2
Plastic, 9, 10, 13-4, 35, 46, 49, 52, 54
Pollen, 52, 60-1
Pollination, 51-2, 54, 73
Pompon type, 7, 14, 18, 42-3, 58, 60, 62, 64, 69, 74
'Buttercup', 18, 74, (13)
'Hallmark', 74
'Linda Harris', 74
'Little Pearl', 74
'Little Sally', 74
'Little Snowdrop', 18, 74, (14)
'Magnificent', 74
'Mark Willo', 18, (12)
'Moore Place', 74
'Mrs Black', 74
'Pam', 74
'Pop Willo', 18, 74, (15)
'Silver Tips', 78
'Small World', 74
'Stoneleigh Joyce', 74
'White Pam', 74
'Willo Cooee', 74
'Willo Fleck', 18, (11)
'Willo's Surprise', 74
Potash, 38-9
Pots, 9, 10-4, 34, 48-9, 50, 71-2
Potting, 11, 13, 49, 50, 54, 71

Potting medium/mixture, 10-13, 34, 49, 50, 54, 71
Pot tubers, 34, 71
Preparation of soil, 15-6
Propagation, 6, 10-4, 54
Pruning, 34, 40-4, 49, 56, 73
Rainwater, 10, 36
Roots, 8-16, 33-8, 40-1, 49-50, 56, 72
Salt, 10, 16, 36, 39, 72
Scalding, 57, 72
Season, 6, 8-15, 33-4, 36, 39-40, 42, 45-6, 48-9, 50-2, 54-5, 71, 73
Seed, 6, 38, 43, 51-4, 71, 73
Seedlings, 6, 7, 14, 34, 51-2, 54, 71
Semi-cactus type, 7, 24-6, 42, 61, 63, 69, 74, 76
Giant:
'Alfred C', 76
'Bramley's Sunset', 76
'Conquistadore', 76
'Elmbrook Rebel', 24, (73)
'Florence Baker', 24, 76, (75)
'Gay Triumph', 24, 76, (74)
'Inca Dambuster', 76
'Maxmann', 24, 76, (71)
'St Joan', 24, 76, (72)
'Sunrise', 76
Large:
'Agricola', 76
'Candy Keene', 24, 76, (78)
'Doc Van Horn', 24, (80)
'Gay Beauty', 24, 76, (76)
'Gay Gertie', 24, 76, (77)
'Gretta', 76
'Kingdown Leader', 76
'Neveric', 76
'Reginald Keene', 24, 76, (79)
'Robbie Huston', 76
'Salmon Keene', 76
'Suffolk Conquest', 76
'Vidale Rhapsody', 76
Medium:
'Autumn Fire', 76
'Bob's Gold', 25, 76, (83)
'Brighton Amber', 76
'Eastwood Pinky', 76
'Formby Sparkle', 25, 76, (85)
'Gay Chieftain', 76
'Gay Peach', 76
'Gay Pride', 25, 76, (81)
'Gay Sunset', 76, (cover)
'Hamari Caprice', 76
'Lavender Gay', 25, 76, (84)
'Libby's Choice', 31, 78, (144)
'Silver Gay', 25, 76, (82)
Small:
'Davenport Sunlight', 76
'Dr J. Fisher', 76
'Gay's Choice', 25, 76, (89)
'Gay's Delight', 25, 76, (86)
'Gay Lollypop', 25, (87)
'Gay Master', 25, 76, (88)
'Gay Snowflake', 76
'Gay Queen', 76
'Kiwi Brother', 76
'Sharrowean Pride', 76
'Whiston Sunrise', 25, (90)
Miniature:
'Alma Dryden', 76
'Brian's First', 26, 76, (94)
'Elaine Gay', 26, 76, (91)
'Gay Faye', 76

'Gay Prince', 26, 76, (93)
'Jean', 26, 76, (92)
'Jean Wanless', 76
'Leslie', 76
'Match', 26, 76, (95)
'Polly', 76
'Rufus', 76
'Twinkletoes', 76
Serrated, 61
Shade, 33, 34, 45-7, 72
Showmanship, 59
Show and Fancy type, 7, *see* Ball type
Shows, 6, 32, 40, 42, 44, 46-7, 57-9, 62, 69, 72, (149-60)
Shrinkage, 9, 71
Single type, 7
Side shoots, 40, 42, 44, 49
Size, 6, 14, 33, 38, 40-2, 48-9, 54, 57-9, 62, 64-5, 68-70, 72, 74-8
Soft-wooded, 10, 40, 44
Soil, 11-2, 15-6, 33-8, 44, 49-50, 54-5, 71-2, 74
Soilless, 50
Soil pH balance, 12, 15, 71
Sport, 67
Species, 7, 13, 51-2
Specimen blooms, 48, 59, 62-5, 69
Staging, 57-9, 65
Stake, 6, 8-9, 14, 16, 33, 41, 45-7, 49, 50, 54, 58, 72
Standard, 6, 7, 51-2, 54, 58-65, 69
Stellar type, 19, 42, 60, 63, 70, 74
'Acacia Julie', 19, 74, (24)
'Acacia Pink', 74
'Acacia Yellow', 74
'Christie Jess', 19, 74, (22)
'Jescot Julie', 19, 74, (23)
'Jescot Lyca', 19, (21)
'Pink Giraffe', 19, (25)
Stem/stalk, 7, 8, 12-4, 38, 40-3, 45, 49, 51, 57-9, 64, 71-2
Stock plants, 11-3, 48-50, 72
Stopping, 12, 40-2, 49-50, 58, 72
Storing tubers, 8, 9, 34, 38, 50-1, 71-3
Substance, 51, 64
Sulphur, 8, 9, 15, 39, 55, 71
Temperature, 10-1, 13, 33, 35-6, 44, 47, 50, 52
Texture, 51, 64
Tie, 8, 41-2, 45, 49-51
Timing, 42, 44, 48
Top cutting, 11
Trace elements, 38-9, 50
Transpiration, 10, 35-6
Trellis, 33
Tropics, 11-3, 33, 48, 54, 71-3
Tubers, 6, 8-11, 13-5, 33-4, 38-9, 48, 50-1, 54-6, 71-3
Tying, 8, 41, 45, 49-51
Type, 6, 7, 14, 17-32, 40, 42-3, 48, 51-2, 54, 58-65, 68-70, 74-8
Viral diseases/virus, 6, 55-6, 72
Wash off, 10, 11, 34-5
Water, 8-13, 16, 33-8, 44, 46, 49-50, 55, 58, 71-3
Watershoots, 41, 72
Weeds/weed control, 37, 55, 72
Wire, 33, 43, 46-7, 57